GOOD NEWS
TOLD BY LUKE

Today's English Version

THE BRITISH AND
FOREIGN BIBLE SOCIETY

THE NATIONAL BIBLE
SOCIETY OF SCOTLAND

in association with
COLLINS
Fontana Books

PRICE 4p

This price is made possible
by the subsidy of the Bible Societies

English—Luke TEV—560P
BFBS/NBSS—1972(2)—100M
ISBN 0 564 06521 8

© *American Bible Society, New York*
1966

Printed in Great Britain
Collins Clear-Type Press
London and Glasgow

LUKE

Introduction

1 Dear Theophilus:
Many have done their best to write a report of the things that have taken place among us. [2] They wrote what we have been told by those who saw these things from the beginning and proclaimed the message. [3] And so, your Excellency, because I have carefully studied all these matters from their beginning, I thought it good to write an orderly account for you. [4] I do this so that you will know the full truth of all those matters which you have been taught.

The Birth of John the Baptist Announced

[5] During the time when Herod was king of Judea, there was a priest named Zechariah, who belonged to the priestly order of Abiah. His wife's name was Elizabeth; she also belonged to a priestly family. [6] They both lived good lives in God's sight, and obeyed fully all the Lord's commandments and rules. [7] They had no children because Elizabeth could not have any, and she and Zechariah were both very old.

[8] One day Zechariah was doing his work as a priest before God, taking his turn in the daily service. [9] According to the custom followed by the priests, he was chosen by lot to burn the incense on the altar. So he went into the Temple of the Lord, [10] while the crowd of people outside prayed during the hour of burning the incense. [11] An

angel of the Lord appeared to him, standing at the right side of the altar where the incense was burned. [12] When Zechariah saw him he was troubled and felt afraid. [13] But the angel said to him: "Don't be afraid, Zechariah! God has heard your prayer, and your wife Elizabeth will bear you a son. You are to name him John. [14] How glad and happy you will be, and how happy many others will be when he is born! [15] For he will be a great man in the Lord's sight. He must not drink any wine or strong drink. From his very birth he will be filled with the Holy Spirit. [16] He will bring back many of the people of Israel to the Lord their God. [17] He will go as God's messenger, strong and mighty like the prophet Elijah. He will bring fathers and children together again; he will turn the disobedient people back to the way of thinking of the righteous; he will get the Lord's people ready for him."

[18] Zechariah said to the angel, "How shall I know if this is so? I am an old man and my wife also is old." [19] "I am Gabriel," the angel answered. "I stand in the presence of God, who sent me to speak to you and tell you this good news. [20] But you have not believed my message, which will come true at the right time. Because you have not believed you will be unable to speak; you will remain silent until the day my promise to you comes true."

[21] In the meantime the people were waiting for Zechariah, wondering why he was spending such a long time in the Temple. [22] When he came out he could not speak to them — and so they knew that he had seen a vision in the Temple. Unable to say a word, he made signs to them with his hands.

[23] When his period of service in the Temple was over, Zechariah went back home. [24] Some time later his wife Elizabeth became pregnant, and did not leave the house for five months. [25] "Now at last the Lord has helped me in this way," she said. "He has taken away my public disgrace!"

The Birth of Jesus Announced

[26] In the sixth month of Elizabeth's pregnancy God sent the angel Gabriel to a town in Galilee named Nazareth. [27] He had a message for a girl promised in marriage to a man named Joseph, who was a descendant of King David.

The girl's name was Mary. ²⁸ The angel came to her and said, "Peace be with you! The Lord is with you, and has greatly blessed you!" ²⁹ Mary was deeply troubled by the angel's message, and she wondered what his words meant. ³⁰ The angel said to her: "Don't be afraid, Mary, for God has been gracious to you. ³¹ You will become pregnant and give birth to a son, and you will name him Jesus. ³² He will be great and will be called the Son of the Most High God. The Lord God will make him a king, as his ancestor David was, ³³ and he will be the king of the descendants of Jacob for ever; his kingdom will never end!"

³⁴ Mary said to the angel, "I am a virgin. How, then, can this be?" ³⁵ The angel answered: "The Holy Spirit will come on you, and God's power will rest upon you. For this reason the holy child will be called the Son of God. ³⁶ Remember your relative Elizabeth. It is said that she cannot have children; but she herself is now six months pregnant, even though she is very old. ³⁷ For there is not a thing that God cannot do."

³⁸ "I am the Lord's servant," said Mary; "may it happen to me as you have said." And the angel left her.

Mary Visits Elizabeth

³⁹ Soon afterward Mary got ready and hurried off to the hill country, to a town in Judea. ⁴⁰ She went into Zechariah's house and greeted Elizabeth. ⁴¹ When Elizabeth heard Mary's greeting, the baby moved within her. Elizabeth was filled with the Holy Spirit, ⁴² and spoke in a loud voice: "Blessed are you among women! Blessed is the child you will bear! ⁴³ Why should this great thing happen to me, that my Lord's mother comes to visit me? ⁴⁴ For as soon as I heard your greeting, the baby within me jumped with gladness. ⁴⁵ How happy are you to believe that the Lord's message to you will come true!"

Mary's Song of Praise

⁴⁶ Mary said:

"My heart praises the Lord,
⁴⁷ My soul is glad because of God my Saviour.
⁴⁸ For he has remembered me, his lowly servant!

And from now on all people will call me
blessed,
⁴⁹ Because of the great things the Mighty God
has done for me.
His name is holy;
⁵⁰ He shows mercy to all who fear him,
From one generation to another.
⁵¹ He stretched out his mighty arm
And scattered the proud people with all their
plans.
⁵² He brought down mighty kings from their
thrones,
And lifted up the lowly.
⁵³ He filled the hungry with good things,
And sent the rich away with empty hands.
⁵⁴ He kept the promise he made to our ancestors;
He came to the help of his servant Israel,
⁵⁵ And remembered to show mercy to Abraham
And to all his descendants for ever!"

⁵⁶ Mary stayed about three months with Elizabeth, and
then went back home.

The Birth of John the Baptist

⁵⁷ The time came for Elizabeth to have her baby, and
she gave birth to a son. ⁵⁸ Her neighbours and relatives
heard how wonderfully good the Lord had been to her,
and they all rejoiced with her.

⁵⁹ When the baby was a week old they came to circum-
cise him; they were going to name him Zechariah, his
father's name. ⁶⁰ But his mother said, "No! His name will
be John." ⁶¹ They said to her, "But you don't have a single
relative with that name!" ⁶² Then they made signs to his
father, asking him what name he would like the boy to
have. ⁶³ Zechariah asked for a writing pad and wrote, "His
name is John." How surprised they all were! ⁶⁴ At that
moment Zechariah was able to speak again, and he started
praising God. ⁶⁵ The neighbours were all filled with fear,
and the news about these things spread through all the hill
country of Judea. ⁶⁶ All who heard of it thought about it
and asked, "What is this child going to be?" For it was
plain that the Lord's power was with him.

Zechariah's Prophecy

⁶⁷ His father Zechariah was filled with the Holy Spirit,
and he prophesied:

⁶⁸ "Let us praise the Lord, the God of Israel!
For he came to the help of his people and set
them free.

⁶⁹ He raised up a mighty Saviour for us,
One who is a descendant of his servant David.

⁷⁰ This is what he said long ago by means of his
holy prophets:

⁷¹ He promised to save us from our enemies,
And from the power of all those who hate us.

⁷² He said he would show mercy to our ancestors,
And remember his sacred covenant.

⁷³⁻⁷⁴ He made a solemn promise to our ancestor
Abraham,
And vowed that he would rescue us from our
enemies,
And allow us to serve him without fear,

⁷⁵ To be holy and righteous before him,
All the days of our life.

⁷⁶ You, my child, will be called a prophet of the
Most High God;
You will go ahead of the Lord
To prepare his road for him,

⁷⁷ To tell his people that they will be saved,
By having their sins forgiven.

⁷⁸ For our God is merciful and tender;
He will cause the bright dawn of salvation to
rise on us,

⁷⁹ And shine from heaven on all those who live
in the dark shadow of death,
To guide our steps into the path of peace."

⁸⁰ The child grew and developed in body and spirit; he
lived in the desert until the day when he would appear
publicly to the people of Israel.

The Birth of Jesus
(Also Matt. 1.18–25)

2 At that time Emperor Augustus sent out an order for
all the citizens of the Empire to register themselves
for the census. ² When this first census took place, Quiri-

nius was the governor of Syria. ³ Everyone, then, went to register himself, each to his own town.

⁴ Joseph went from the town of Nazareth, in Galilee, to Judea, to the town named Bethlehem, where King David was born. Joseph went there because he himself was a descendant of David. ⁵ He went to register himself with

Mary, who was promised in marriage to him. She was pregnant, ⁶ and while they were in Bethlehem, the time came for her to have her baby. ⁷ She gave birth to her first son, wrapped him in cloths and laid him in a manger — there was no room for them to stay in the inn.

The Shepherds and the Angels

⁸ There were some shepherds in that part of the country who were spending the night in the fields, taking care of their flocks. ⁹ An angel of the Lord appeared to them, and the glory of the Lord shone over them. They were terribly afraid, ¹⁰ but the angel said to them: "Don't be afraid! For I am here with good news for you, which will bring great joy to all the people. ¹¹ This very night in David's town your Saviour was born — Christ the Lord! ¹² This is what will prove it to you: you will find a baby wrapped in cloths and lying in a manger."

¹³ Suddenly a great army of heaven's angels appeared with the angel, singing praises to God:

¹⁴ "Glory to God in the highest heaven!
    And peace on earth to men with whom he is
        pleased!"

15 When the angels went away from them back into heaven, the shepherds said to one another, "Let us go to Bethlehem and see this thing that has happened, that the Lord has told us." 16 So they hurried off and found Mary and Joseph, and saw the baby lying in the manger. 17 When the shepherds saw him they told them what the angel had said about this child. 18 All who heard it were filled with wonder at what the shepherds told them. 19 Mary remembered all these things, and thought deeply about them. 20 The shepherds went back, singing praises to God for all they had heard and seen; it had been just as the angel had told them.

Jesus Is Named

21 A week later, when the time came for the baby to be circumcised, he was named Jesus — the name which the angel had given him before he had been conceived.

Jesus Is Presented in the Temple

22 The time came for Joseph and Mary to do what the Law of Moses commanded and perform the ceremony of purification. So they took the child to Jerusalem to present him to the Lord. 23 This is what is written in the law of the Lord: "Every first-born male shall be dedicated to

the Lord." 24 They also went to offer a sacrifice as required by the law of the Lord: "A pair of doves or two young pigeons."

25 Now there was a man living in Jerusalem whose name was Simeon. He was a good and God-fearing man, and was waiting for Israel to be saved. The Holy Spirit was with him, 26 and he had been assured by the Holy Spirit that he would not die before he had seen the Lord's promised Messiah. 27 Led by the Spirit, Simeon went into the Temple. When the parents brought the child Jesus into the Temple to do for him what the Law required, 28 Simeon took the child in his arms, and gave thanks to God:

29 "Now, Lord, you have kept your promise,
     And you may let your servant go in peace.
30 For with my own eyes I have seen your salvation,
31 Which you have made ready in the presence
     of all peoples:
32 A light to reveal your way to the Gentiles,
     And to give glory to your people Israel."

33 The child's father and mother were amazed at the things Simeon said about him. 34 Simeon blessed them and said to Mary, his mother: "This child is chosen by God for the destruction and the salvation of many in Israel; he will be a sign from God which many people will speak against, 35 and so reveal their secret thoughts. And sorrow, like a sharp sword, will break your own heart."

36 There was a prophetess named Anna, daughter of Phanuel, of the tribe of Asher. She was an old woman who had been married for seven years, 37 and then had been a widow for eighty-four years. She never left the Temple; day and night she worshipped God, fasting and praying. 38 That very same hour she arrived and gave thanks to God, and spoke about the child to all who were waiting for God to redeem Jerusalem.

The Return to Nazareth

39 When they finished doing all that was required by the law of the Lord, they returned to Galilee, to their home town of Nazareth. 40 And the child grew and became strong; he was full of wisdom, and God's blessings were with him.

The Boy Jesus in the Temple

⁴¹ Every year Jesus' parents went to Jerusalem for the Feast of Passover. ⁴² When Jesus was twelve years old, they went to the feast as usual. ⁴³ When the days of the feast were over, they started back home, but the boy Jesus stayed in Jerusalem. His parents did not know this; ⁴⁴ they thought that he was with the group, so they travelled a whole day, and then started looking for him among their relatives and friends. ⁴⁵ They did not find him, so they went back to Jerusalem looking for him. ⁴⁶ On the third day they found him in the Temple, sitting with the Jewish teachers, listening to them and asking questions. ⁴⁷ All

who heard him were amazed at his intelligent answers. ⁴⁸ His parents were amazed when they saw him, and his mother said to him, "Son, why did you do this to us? Your father and I have been terribly worried trying to find you." ⁴⁹ He answered them, "Why did you have to look for me? Didn't you know that I had to be in my Father's house?" ⁵⁰ But they did not understand what he said to them.

⁵¹ So Jesus went back with them to Nazareth, where he was obedient to them. His mother treasured all these things in her heart. ⁵² And Jesus grew up, both in body and in wisdom, gaining favour with God and men.

The Preaching of John the Baptist
(Also Matt. 3.1–12; Mark 1.1–8; John 1.19–28)

3 It was the fifteenth year of the rule of Emperor Tiberius; Pontius Pilate was governor of Judea, Herod was ruler of Galilee, and his brother Philip ruler of the territory of Iturea and Trachonitis; Lysanias was ruler of Abilene, ² and Annas and Caiaphas were high priests. It was at this time that the word of God came to John, the son of Zechariah, in the desert. ³ So John went throughout the whole territory of the Jordan river. "Turn away from your sins and be baptized," he preached, "and God will forgive your sins." ⁴ As the prophet Isaiah had written in his book:

"Someone is shouting in the desert:
'Get the Lord's road ready for him,
Make a straight path for him to travel!
⁵ All low places must be filled up,
All hills and mountains levelled off;
The winding roads must be made straight,
The rough paths made smooth;
⁶ And all mankind will see God's salvation!'"

⁷ Crowds of people came out to John to be baptized by him. "You snakes!" he said to them. "Who told you that you could escape from God's wrath that is about to come? ⁸ Do the things that will show that you have turned from your sins. And don't start saying among yourselves, 'Abraham is our ancestor.' I tell you that God can take these rocks and make descendants for Abraham! ⁹ The axe is ready to cut the trees down at the roots; every tree that does not bear good fruit will be cut down and thrown in the fire."

¹⁰ The people asked him, "What are we to do, then?" ¹¹ He answered, "Whoever has two shirts must give one to the man who has none, and whoever has food must share it." ¹² Some tax collectors came to be baptized, and they asked him, "Teacher, what are we to do?" ¹³ "Don't collect more than is legal," he told them. ¹⁴ Some soldiers also asked him, "What about us? What are we to do?" He said to them, "Don't take money from anyone by force or by false charges; be content with your pay."

¹⁵ People's hopes began to rise; and they began to wonder about John, thinking that perhaps he might be the Messiah. ¹⁶ So John said to all of them: "I baptize you with water, but one who is much greater than I is coming.

I am not good enough even to untie his sandals. He will baptize you with the Holy Spirit and fire. ¹⁷ He has his winnowing-shovel with him, to thresh out all the grain and gather the wheat into his barn; but he will burn the chaff in a fire that never goes out!'

¹⁸ In many different ways John urged the people as he preached the Good News to them. ¹⁹ But John spoke against Governor Herod, because he had married Herodias, his brother's wife, and had done many other evil things. ²⁰ Then Herod did an even worse thing by putting John in prison.

The Baptism of Jesus
(Also Matt. 3.13–17; Mark 1.9–11)

²¹ After all the people had been baptized, Jesus also was baptized. While he was praying, heaven was opened, ²² and the Holy Spirit came down upon him in bodily form, like a dove. And a voice came from heaven: "You are my own dear Son. I am well pleased with you."

The Genealogy of Jesus
(Also Matt. 1.1–17)

²³ When Jesus began his work he was about thirty years old; he was the son, so people thought, of Joseph, who was the son of Heli, ²⁴ the son of Matthat, the son of Levi, the son of Melchi, the son of Jannai, the son of Joseph, ²⁵ the son of Mattathias, the son of Amos, the son of Nahum, the son of Esli, the son of Naggai, ²⁶ the son of Maath, the son of Mattathias, the son of Semein, the son of Josech, the son of Joda, ²⁷ the son of Joanan, the son of Rhesa, the son of Zerubbabel, the son of Shealtiel, the son of Neri, ²⁸ the son of Melchi, the son of Addi, the son of Cosam, the son of Elmadam, the son of Er, ²⁹ the son of Joshua, the son of Eliezer, the son of Jorim, the son of Matthat, the son of Levi, ³⁰ the son of Simeon, the son of Judah, the son of Joseph, the son of Jonam, the son of Eliakim, ³¹ the son of Melea, the son of Menna, the son of Mattatha, the son of Nathan, the son of David, ³² the son of Jesse, the son of Obed, the son of Boaz, the son of Salmon, the son of Nahshon, ³³ the son of Amminadab, the son of Admin, the son of Arni, the son of Hezron, the son of Perez, the son of Judah, ³⁴ the son of Jacob, the son of Isaac, the son of Abraham, the son of Terah, the son of Nahor,

³⁵ the son of Serug, the son of Reu, the son of Peleg, the son of Eber, the son of Shelah, ³⁶ the son of Cainan, the son of Arphaxad, the son of Shem, the son of Noah, the son of Lamech, ³⁷ the son of Methuselah, the son of Enoch, the son of Jared, the son of Mahalaleel, the son of Cainan, ³⁸ the son of Enos, the son of Seth, the son of Adam, the son of God.

The Temptation of Jesus
(Also Matt. 4.1–11; Mark 1.12–13)

4 Jesus returned from the Jordan full of the Holy Spirit, and was led by the Spirit into the desert, ² where he was tempted by the Devil for forty days. He ate nothing all that time, so that he was hungry when it was over.

³ The Devil said to him, "If you are God's Son, order this stone to turn into bread." ⁴ Jesus answered, "The scripture says, 'Man cannot live on bread alone.'"

⁵ Then the Devil took him up and showed him in a second all the kingdoms of the world. ⁶ "I will give you all this power, and all this wealth," the Devil told him. "It was all handed over to me and I can give it to anyone I choose. ⁷ All this will be yours, then, if you kneel down before me." ⁸ Jesus answered, "The scripture says, 'Worship the Lord your God and serve only him!'"

⁹ Then the Devil took him to Jerusalem and set him on the highest point of the Temple, and said to him, "If you are God's Son, throw yourself down from here. ¹⁰ For the scripture says, 'God will order his angels to take good care of you.' ¹¹ It also says, 'They will hold you up with their hands so that you will not even hurt your feet on the stones.'" ¹² Jesus answered him, "The scripture says, 'You must not put the Lord your God to the test.'" ¹³ When the Devil finished tempting Jesus in every way, he left him for a while.

Jesus Begins His Work in Galilee
(Also Matt. 4.12–17; Mark 1.14–15)

¹⁴ Then Jesus returned to Galilee, and the power of the Holy Spirit was with him. The news about him spread throughout all that territory. ¹⁵ He taught in their synagogues and was praised by all.

Jesus Rejected at Nazareth
(Also Matt. 13.53–58; Mark 6.1–6)

¹⁶ Then Jesus went to Nazareth, where he had been brought up, and on the Sabbath day he went as usual to the synagogue. He stood up to read the Scriptures, ¹⁷ and was handed the book of the prophet Isaiah. He unrolled the scroll and found the place where it is written:

¹⁸ "The Spirit of the Lord is upon me.
He has anointed me to preach the Good News to the poor,
He has sent me to proclaim liberty to the captives,
And recovery of sight to the blind,
To set free the oppressed,
¹⁹ To announce the year when the Lord will save his people!"

²⁰ Jesus rolled up the scroll, gave it back to the attendant, and sat down. All the people in the synagogue had their eyes fixed on him. ²¹ He began speaking to them: "This passage of scripture has come true today, as you heard it being read." ²² They were all well impressed with him, and marvelled at the beautiful words that he spoke. They said, "Isn't he the son of Joseph?" ²³ He said to them: "I am sure that you will quote the proverb to me, 'Doctor, heal yourself.' You will also say to me, 'Do here in your own home town the same things we were told happened in Capernaum.' ²⁴ I tell you this," Jesus added: "A prophet is never welcomed in his own home town. ²⁵ Listen to me: it is true that there were many widows in Israel during the time of Elijah, when there was no rain for three and a half years and there was a great famine throughout the whole land. ²⁶ Yet Elijah was not sent to a single one of them, but only to a widow of Zarephath, in the territory of Sidon. ²⁷ And there were many lepers in Israel during the time of the prophet Elisha; yet not one of them was made clean, but only Naaman the Syrian." ²⁸ All the people in the synagogue were filled with anger when they heard this. ²⁹ They rose up, dragged Jesus out of town, and took him to the top of the hill on which their town was built, to throw him over the cliff. ³⁰ But he walked through the middle of the crowd and went his way.

A Man with an Evil Spirit
(Also Mark 1.21–28)

³¹ Then Jesus went to Capernaum, a town in Galilee, where he taught the people on the Sabbath. ³² They were all amazed at the way he taught, for his words had authority. ³³ There was a man in the synagogue who had the spirit of an evil demon in him; he screamed out in a loud voice: ³⁴ "Ah! What do you want with us, Jesus of Nazareth? Are you here to destroy us? I know who you are: you are God's holy messenger!" ³⁵ Jesus commanded the spirit: "Be quiet, and come out of the man!" The demon threw the man down in front of them all, and went out of him without doing him any harm. ³⁶ Everyone was amazed, and they said to one another: "What kind of word is this? With authority and power this man gives orders to the evil spirits, and they come out!" ³⁷ And the report about Jesus spread everywhere in that region.

Jesus Heals Many People
(Also Matt. 8.14–17; Mark 1.29–34)

³⁸ Jesus left the synagogue and went to Simon's home. Simon's mother-in-law was sick with a high fever, and they spoke to Jesus about her. ³⁹ He went and stood at her bedside, and gave a command to the fever. The fever left her and she got up at once and began to wait on them.

⁴⁰ After sunset, all who had friends who were sick with various diseases brought them to Jesus; he placed his hands on every one of them and healed them all. ⁴¹ Demons, also, went out from many people, screaming, "You are the Son of God!" Jesus commanded them and would not let them speak, because they knew that he was the Messiah.

Jesus Preaches in Judea
(Also Mark 1.35–39)

⁴² At daybreak Jesus left the town and went off to a lonely place. The people started looking for him, and when they found him they tried to keep him from leaving. ⁴³ But he said to them, "I must preach the Good News of the Kingdom of God in other towns also, for that is what God sent me to do." ⁴⁴ So he preached in the synagogues of Judea.

Jesus Calls the First Disciples
(Also Matt. 4.18–22; Mark 1.16–20)

5 One time Jesus was standing on the shore of Lake
Gennesaret while the people pushed their way up to
him to listen to the word of God. ² He saw two boats
pulled up on the beach; the fishermen had left them and
gone off to wash the nets. ³ Jesus got into one of the boats
—it belonged to Simon—and asked him to push off a little
from the shore. Jesus sat in the boat and taught the
crowd.

⁴ When he finished speaking, he said to Simon, "Push
the boat out further to the deep water, and you and your
partners let your nets down for a catch." ⁵ "Master,"
Simon answered, "we worked hard all night long and
caught nothing. But if you say so, I will let down the
nets." ⁶ They let the nets down and caught such a large
number of fish that the nets were about to break. ⁷ So
they motioned to their partners in the other boat to come
and help them. They came and filled both boats so full
of fish that they were about to sink. ⁸ When Simon Peter
saw what had happened, he fell on his knees before Jesus
and said, "Go away from me, Lord, for I am a sinful
man!" ⁹ He and all the others with him were amazed at
the large number of fish they had caught. ¹⁰ The same was
true of Simon's partners, James and John, the sons of
Zebedee. Jesus said to Simon, "Don't be afraid; from now
on you will be catching men." ¹¹ They pulled the boats on
the beach, left everything and followed Jesus.

Jesus Makes a Leper Clean
(Also Matt. 8.1–4; Mark 1.40–45)

¹² Once Jesus was in a certain town where there was a man who was covered with leprosy. When he saw Jesus, he fell on his face before him and begged, "Sir, if you want to, you can make me clean!" ¹³ Jesus reached out and touched him. "I do want to," he said. "Be clean!" At once the leprosy left the man. ¹⁴ Jesus ordered him, "Don't tell this to anyone, but go straight to the priest and let him examine you; then offer the sacrifice, as Moses ordered, to prove to everyone that you are now clean." ¹⁵ But the news about Jesus spread all the more widely, and crowds of people came to hear him and be healed from their diseases. ¹⁶ But he would go away to lonely places, where he prayed.

Jesus Heals a Paralyzed Man
(Also Matt. 9.1–8; Mark 2.1–12)

¹⁷ One day when Jesus was teaching, some Pharisees and teachers of the Law were sitting there who had come from every town in Galilee and Judea, and from Jerusalem. The power of the Lord was present for Jesus to heal the sick. ¹⁸ Some men came carrying a paralyzed man on a bed, and they tried to take him into the house and lay him before Jesus. ¹⁹ Because of the crowd, however, they could find no way to take him in. So they carried him up on the roof, made an opening in the tiles, and let him down on his bed into the middle of the group in front of Jesus.

20 When Jesus saw how much faith they had, he said to the man, "Your sins are forgiven you, my friend." 21 The teachers of the Law and the Pharisees began to say to themselves: "Who is this man who speaks against God in this way? No man can forgive sins; God alone can!" 22 Jesus knew their thoughts and said to them: "Why do you think such things? 23 Is it easier to say, 'Your sins are forgiven you,' or to say, 'Get up and walk'? 24 I will prove to you, then, that the Son of Man has authority on earth to forgive sins." So he said to the paralyzed man, "I tell you, get up, pick up your bed, and go home!" 25 At once the man got up before them all, took the bed he had been lying on, and went home, praising God. 26 They were all completely amazed! Full of fear, they praised God, saying, "What marvellous things we have seen today!"

Jesus Calls Levi
(Also Matt. 9.9–13; Mark 2.13–17)

27 After this, Jesus went out and saw a tax collector named Levi, sitting in his office. Jesus said to him, "Follow me." 28 Levi got up, left everything and followed him.

29 Then Levi had a big feast in his house for Jesus, and there was a large number of tax collectors and other people sitting with them. 30 Some Pharisees and teachers of the Law who belonged to their group complained to Jesus' disciples. "Why do you eat and drink with tax collectors and outcasts?" they asked. 31 Jesus answered them: "People who are well do not need a doctor, but only those who are sick. 32 I have not come to call the respectable people to repent, but the outcasts."

The Question about Fasting
(Also Matt. 9.14–17; Mark 2.18–22)

33 Some people said to Jesus, "The disciples of John fast frequently and offer up prayers, and the disciples of the Pharisees do the same; but your disciples eat and drink." 34 Jesus answered: "Do you think you can make the guests at a wedding party go without food as long as the bridegroom is with them? Of course not! 35 But the time will come when the bridegroom will be taken away from them, and they will go without food in those days."

36 Jesus told them this parable also: "No one tears a piece off a new coat to patch up an old coat. If he does,

he will have torn the new coat, and the piece of new cloth will not match the old. ³⁷ Nor does anyone pour new wine into used wineskins. If he does, the new wine will burst the skins, the wine will pour out, and the skins will be ruined. ³⁸ No! New wine should be poured into fresh skins! ³⁹ And no one wants new wine after drinking old wine. 'The old is better,' he says."

The Question about the Sabbath
(Also Matt. 12.1–8; Mark 2.23–28)

6 Jesus was walking through some wheat fields on a Sabbath day. His disciples began to pick the heads of wheat, rub them in their hands, and eat the grain. ² Some Pharisees said, "Why are you doing what our Law says you cannot do on the Sabbath?" ³ Jesus answered them: "Haven't you read what David did when he and his men were hungry? ⁴ He went into the house of God, took the bread offered to God, ate it, and gave it also to his men. Yet it is against our Law for anyone to eat it except the priests." ⁵ And Jesus added, "The Son of Man is Lord of the Sabbath."

The Man with a Crippled Hand
(Also Matt. 12.9–14; Mark 3.1–6)

⁶ On another Sabbath Jesus went into a synagogue and taught. A man was there whose right hand was crippled. ⁷ Some teachers of the Law and Pharisees wanted some reason to accuse Jesus of doing wrong; so they watched him very closely to see if he would cure anyone on the Sabbath. ⁸ But Jesus knew their thoughts and said to the man with the crippled hand, "Stand up and come here to the front." The man got up and stood there. ⁹ Then Jesus said to them: "I ask you: What does our Law allow us to do on the Sabbath? To help or to harm? To save a man's life or destroy it?" ¹⁰ He looked around at them all, then said to the man, "Stretch out your hand." He did so, and his hand became well again. ¹¹ But they were filled with rage and began to discuss among themselves what they could do to Jesus.

Jesus Chooses the Twelve Apostles
(Also Matt. 10.1–4; Mark 3.13–19)

¹² At that time Jesus went up a hill to pray, and spent

the whole night there praying to God. ¹³ When day came he called his disciples to him and chose twelve of them, whom he named apostles: ¹⁴ Simon (whom he also named Peter) and his brother Andrew; James and John, Philip and Bartholomew, ¹⁵ Matthew and Thomas, James the son of Alphaeus and Simon (who was called the patriot), ¹⁶ Judas the son of James and Judas Iscariot, who became the traitor.

Jesus Teaches and Heals
(Also Matt. 4.23–25)

¹⁷ Coming down from the hill with them, Jesus stood on a level place with a large number of his disciples. A great crowd of people was there from all over Judea, and from Jerusalem, and from the coast cities of Tyre and Sidon; ¹⁸ they came to hear him and to be healed of their diseases. Those who were troubled by evil spirits also came and were healed. ¹⁹ All the people tried to touch him, for power was going out from him and healing them all.

Happiness and Sorrow
(Also Matt. 5.1–12)

²⁰ Jesus looked at his disciples and said:
   "Happy are you poor:
      the Kingdom of God is yours!
²¹ "Happy are you who are hungry now:
      you will be filled!
   "Happy are you who weep now:
      you will laugh!
²² "Happy are you when men hate you, and reject you, and insult you, and say that you are evil, because of the Son of Man! ²³ Be happy when that happens, and dance for joy, for a great reward is kept for you in heaven. For their ancestors did the very same things to the prophets.
²⁴ "But how terrible for you who are rich now:
      you have had your easy life!
²⁵ "How terrible for you who are full now:
      you will go hungry!
   "How terrible for you who laugh now:
      you will mourn and weep!
²⁶ "How terrible when all men speak well of you; for their ancestors said the very same things to the false prophets."

Love for Enemies
(Also Matt. 5.38–48; 7.12a)

27 "But I tell you who hear me: Love your enemies, do good to those who hate you, 28 bless those who curse you, and pray for those who mistreat you. 29 If anyone hits you on the cheek, let him hit the other one too; if someone takes your coat, let him have your shirt as well. 30 Give to everyone who asks you for something, and when someone takes what is yours, do not ask for it back. 31 Do for others just what you want them to do for you.

32 "If you love only the people who love you, why should you expect a blessing? Even sinners love those who love them! 33 And if you do good only to those who do good to you, why should you expect a blessing? Even sinners do that! 34 And if you lend only to those from whom you hope to get it back, why should you expect a blessing? Even sinners lend to sinners, to get back the same amount! 35 No! Love your enemies and do good to them; lend and expect nothing back. You will have a great

reward, and you will be sons of the Most High God. For he is good to the ungrateful and the wicked.' 36 Be merciful, just as your Father is merciful."

Judging Others
(Also Matt. 7.1–5)

37 "Do not judge others, and God will not judge you; do not condemn others, and God will not condemn you; forgive others, and God will forgive you. 38 Give to others, and God will give to you: you will receive a full measure, a generous helping, poured into your hands — all that you

can hold. The measure you use for others is the one God will use for you."

39 And Jesus told them this parable: "One blind man cannot lead another one; if he does, both will fall into a ditch. 40 No pupil is greater than his teacher; but every pupil, when he has completed his training, will be like his teacher.

41 "Why do you look at the speck in your brother's eye, but pay no attention to the log in your own eye? 42 How can you say to your brother, 'Please, brother, let me take that speck out of your eye,' yet not even see the log in your own eye? You impostor! Take the log out of your own eye first, and then you will be able to see and take the speck out of your brother's eye."

A Tree and its Fruit
(Also Matt. 7.16–20; 12.33–35)

43 "A healthy tree does not bear bad fruit, nor does a poor tree bear good fruit. 44 Every tree is known by the fruit it bears; you do not pick figs from thorn bushes, or gather grapes from bramble bushes. 45 A good man brings good out of the treasure of good things in his heart; a bad man brings bad out of his treasure of bad things. For a man's mouth speaks what his heart is full of."

The Two House Builders
(Also Matt. 7.24–27)

46 "Why do you call me, 'Lord, Lord,' and don't do what I tell you? 47 Everyone who comes to me, and listens to my words, and obeys them — I will show you what he is like. 48 He is like a man who built a house: he dug deep and laid the foundation on the rock. The river flooded over and hit that house but it could not shake it, because the house had been well built. 49 But the one who hears my words and does not obey them is like a man who built a house on the ground without laying a foundation; when the flood hit that house it fell at once — what a terrible crash that was!"

Jesus Heals a Roman Officer's Servant
(Also Matt. 8.5–13)

7 When Jesus had finished saying all these things to the people, he went to Capernaum. 2 A Roman officer

there had a servant who was very dear to him; the man was sick and about to die. ³ When the officer heard about Jesus, he sent to him some Jewish elders to ask him to come and heal his servant. ⁴ They came to Jesus and begged him earnestly: "This man really deserves your help. ⁵ He loves our people and he himself built a synagogue for us." ⁶ So Jesus went with them. He was not far from the house when the officer sent friends to tell him: "Sir, don't trouble yourself. I do not deserve to have you come into my house, ⁷ neither do I consider myself worthy to come to you in person. Just give the order and my servant will get well. ⁸ I, too, am a man placed under the authority of superior officers, and I have soldiers under me. I order this one, 'Go!' and he goes; I order that one, 'Come!' and he comes; and I order my slave, 'Do this!' and he does it." ⁹ Jesus was surprised when he heard this; he turned around and said to the crowd following him, "I have never found such faith as this, I tell you, not even in Israel!" ¹⁰ The messengers went back to the officer's house and found his servant well.

Jesus Raises a Widow's Son

¹¹ Soon afterward Jesus went to a town named Nain; his disciples and a large crowd went with him. ¹² Just as he arrived at the gate of the town, a funeral procession was coming out. The dead man was the only son of a woman who was a widow, and a large crowd from the city was with her. ¹³ When the Lord saw her his heart was filled with pity for her and he said to her, "Don't cry." ¹⁴ Then he walked over and touched the coffin, and the men carrying it stopped. Jesus said, "Young man! Get up, I tell you!" ¹⁵ The dead man sat up and began to talk, and Jesus gave him back to his mother. ¹⁶ Everyone was filled with fear, and they praised God: "A great prophet has appeared among us!" and, "God has come to save his people!" ¹⁷ This news about Jesus went out through all of Judea and the surrounding territory.

The Messengers from John the Baptist
(Also Matt. 11.2–19)

¹⁸ John's disciples told him about all these things. John called two of them to him ¹⁹ and sent them to the Lord to ask him, "Are you the one John said was going to come,

or should we expect someone else?" ²⁰ When they came to Jesus they said, "John the Baptist sent us to ask, 'Are you the one he said was going to come, or should we expect someone else?'" ²¹ At that very time Jesus healed many people from their sicknesses, diseases, and evil spirits, and gave sight to many blind people. ²² He answered John's messengers: "Go back and tell John what you have seen and heard: the blind can see, the lame can walk, the lepers are made clean, the deaf can hear, the dead are raised to life, and the Good News is preached to the poor. ²³ How happy is he who has no doubts about me!"

²⁴ After John's messengers had left, Jesus began to speak about John to the crowds: "When you went out to John in the desert, what did you expect to see? A blade of grass bending in the wind? ²⁵ What did you go out to see? A man dressed up in fancy clothes? Really, those who dress like that and live in luxury are found in palaces! ²⁶ Tell me, what did you expect to see? A prophet? Yes, I tell you — you saw much more than a prophet. ²⁷ For John is the one of whom the scripture says, 'Here is my messenger, says God; I will send him ahead of you to open the way for you.' ²⁸ I tell you," Jesus added, "John is greater than any man ever born; but he who is least in the Kingdom of God is greater than he."

²⁹ All the people and the tax collectors heard him; they were the ones who had obeyed God's righteous demands and had been baptized by John. ³⁰ But the Pharisees and the teachers of the Law rejected God's purpose for themselves, and refused to be baptized by John.

³¹ "Now, to what can I compare the people of this day? What are they like? ³² They are like children sitting in the market place. One group shouts to the other, 'We played wedding music for you, but you would not dance! We sang funeral songs, but you would not cry!' ³³ John the Baptist came, and he fasted and drank no wine, and you said, 'He is a madman!' ³⁴ The Son of Man came, and he ate and drank, and you said, 'Look at this man! He is a glutton and wine-drinker, and is a friend of tax collectors and outcasts!' ³⁵ God's wisdom, however, is shown to be true by all who accept it."

Jesus at the Home of Simon the Pharisee

³⁶ A Pharisee invited Jesus to have dinner with him.

Jesus went to his house and sat down to eat. ³⁷ There was a woman in that town who lived a sinful life. She heard that Jesus was eating in the Pharisee's house, so she brought an alabaster jar full of perfume ³⁸ and stood behind Jesus, by his feet, crying and wetting his feet with her tears. Then she dried his feet with her hair, kissed them, and poured the perfume on them. ³⁹ When the Pharisee who had invited Jesus saw this, he said to himself, "If this man really were a prophet, he would know who this woman is who is touching him; he would know what kind of sinful life she leads!" ⁴⁰ Jesus spoke up and said to him, "Simon, I have something to tell you." "Yes, Teacher," he said, "tell me." ⁴¹ "There were two men who owed money to a moneylender," Jesus began; "one owed him fifty pounds and the other one five pounds. ⁴² Neither one could pay him back, so he cancelled the debts of both. Which one, then, will love him more?" ⁴³ "I suppose," answered Simon, "that it would be the one who was forgiven more." "Your answer is correct," said Jesus. ⁴⁴ Then he turned to the woman and said to Simon: "Do you see this woman? I came into your home, and you gave me no water for my feet, but she has washed my feet with her tears and dried them with her hair. ⁴⁵ You

did not welcome me with a kiss, but she has not stopped kissing my feet since I came. ⁴⁶ You provided no oil for my head, but she has covered my feet with perfume. ⁴⁷ I

tell you, then, the great love she has shown proves that her
many sins have been forgiven. Whoever has been forgiven
little, however, shows only a little love." ⁴⁸ Then Jesus
said to the woman, "Your sins are forgiven." ⁴⁹ The others
sitting at the table began to say to themselves, "Who is
this, who even forgives sins?" ⁵⁰ But Jesus said to the
woman, "Your faith has saved you; go in peace."

Women who Accompanied Jesus

8 Some time later Jesus made a journey through towns
and villages, preaching the Good News about the
Kingdom of God. The twelve disciples went with him,
² and so did some women who had been healed of evil
spirits and diseases: Mary (who was called Magdalene),
from whom seven demons had been driven out; ³ Joanna,
the wife of Chuza who was an officer in Herod's court;
Susanna, and many other women who helped Jesus and his
disciples with their belongings.

The Parable of the Sower
(Also Matt. 13.1–9; Mark 4.1–9)

⁴ People kept coming to Jesus from one town after
another; and when a great crowd gathered, Jesus told this
parable:
⁵ "A man went out to sow his seed. As he scattered the
seed in the field, some of it fell along the path, where it
was stepped on, and the birds ate it. ⁶ Some of it fell on
rocky ground, and when the plants sprouted they dried up,
because the soil had no moisture. ⁷ Some of the seed fell
among thorns, which grew up with the plants and choked
them. ⁸ And some seeds fell in good soil; the plants grew
and bore grain, one hundred grains each." And Jesus
added, "Listen, then, if you have ears to hear with!"

The Purpose of the Parables
(Also Matt. 13.10–17; Mark 4.10–12)

⁹ His disciples asked Jesus what this parable meant.
¹⁰ Jesus answered, "The knowledge of the secrets of the
Kingdom of God has been given to you; but to the rest it
comes by means of parables, so that they may look but
not see, and listen but not understand."

Jesus Explains the Parable of the Sower
(Also Matt. 13.18–23; Mark 4.13–20)

¹¹ "This is what the parable means: the seed is the word of God. ¹² The seed that fell along the path stands for those who hear; but the Devil comes and takes the message away from their hearts to keep them from believing and being saved. ¹³ The seed that fell on rocky ground stands for those who hear the message and receive it gladly. But it does not sink deep into them; they believe only for a while, and fall away when the time of temptation comes. ¹⁴ The seed that fell among thorns stands for those who hear; but the worries and riches and pleasures of this life crowd in and choke them, and their fruit never ripens. ¹⁵ The seed that fell in good soil stands for those who hear the message and retain it in a good and obedient heart, and persist until they bear fruit."

A Lamp under a Bowl
(Also Mark 4.21–25)

¹⁶ "No one lights a lamp and covers it with a bowl or puts it under a bed. Instead, he puts it on the lamp-stand, so that people will see the light as they come in. ¹⁷ Whatever is hidden away will be brought out into the open, and whatever is covered up will be found and brought to light.

¹⁸ "Be careful, then, how you listen; for whoever has something will be given more, but whoever has nothing will have taken away from him even the little he thinks he has."

Jesus' Mother and Brothers
(Also Matt. 12.46–50; Mark 3.31–35)

¹⁹ Jesus' mother and brothers came to him, but were unable to join him because of the crowd. ²⁰ Someone said to Jesus, "Your mother and brothers are standing outside and want to see you." ²¹ Jesus said to them all, "My mother and brothers are those who hear the word of God and obey it."

Jesus Calms a Storm
(Also Matt. 8.23–27; Mark 4.35–41)

²² One day Jesus got into a boat with his disciples and said to them, "Let us go across to the other side of the lake." So they started out. ²³ As they were sailing, Jesus

went to sleep. A strong wind blew down on the lake, and
the boat began to fill with water, putting them all in great
danger. 24 The disciples came to Jesus and woke him up,
saying, "Master, Master! We are about to die!" Jesus
got up and gave a command to the wind and to the stormy
water; they quietened down and there was a great calm.
25 Then he said to the disciples, "Where is your faith?"
But they were amazed and afraid, and said to one another:
"Who is this man? He gives orders to the winds and
waves, and they obey him!"

Jesus Heals a Man with Demons
(Also Matt. 8.28–34; Mark 5.1–20)

26 They sailed on over to the territory of the Gergesenes,
which is across the lake from Galilee. 27 As Jesus stepped
ashore, he was met by a man from the town who had
demons in him. He had gone for a long time without
clothes, and would not stay at home, but spent his time
in the burial caves. 28 When he saw Jesus he gave a loud
cry, fell down before him and said in a loud voice: "Jesus,
Son of the Most High God! What do you want with me?
I beg you, don't punish me!" 29 He said this because Jesus
had ordered the evil spirit to go out of him. Many times
it had seized him, and even though he was kept a prisoner,
his hands and feet tied with chains, he would break the
chains and be driven by the demon out into the desert.
30 Jesus asked him, "What is your name?" "My name is
'Mob,'" he answered — because many demons had gone
into him. 31 The demons begged Jesus not to send them
into the abyss.

32 A large herd of pigs was near by, feeding on the hill-
side. The demons begged Jesus to let them go into the
pigs — and he let them. 33 So the demons went out of
the man and into the pigs; the whole herd rushed down the
side of the cliff into the lake and were drowned.

34 The men who were taking care of the pigs saw what
happened, so they ran off and spread the news in the town
and among the farms. 35 People went out to see what had
happened. They came to Jesus and found the man from
whom the demons had gone out sitting at the feet of Jesus,
clothed, and in his right mind — and they were all afraid.
36 Those who had seen it told the people how the man had
been cured. 37 Then the whole crowd from the territory

of the Gergesenes asked Jesus to go away, for they were all terribly afraid. So Jesus got into the boat and left. 38 The man from whom the demons had gone out begged Jesus, "Let me go with you." But Jesus sent him away, saying, 39 "Go back home and tell what God has done for you." The man went through the whole town telling what Jesus had done for him.

Jairus' Daughter and the Woman who Touched Jesus' Cloak
(Also Matt. 9.18–26; Mark 5.21–43)

40 When Jesus returned to the other side of the lake the crowd welcomed him, for they had all been waiting for him. 41 Then a man named Jairus arrived, an official in the local synagogue. He threw himself down at Jesus' feet and begged him to go to his home, 42 for his only daughter, twelve years old, was dying.

As Jesus went along, the people were crowding him from every side. 43 A certain woman was there who had suffered from severe bleeding for twelve years; she had spent all she had on doctors, but no one had been able to cure her. 44 She came up in the crowd behind Jesus and touched the edge of his cloak, and her bleeding stopped at once. 45 Jesus asked, "Who touched me?" Everyone denied it, and Peter said, "Master, the people are all around you and crowding in on you." 46 But Jesus said, "Someone touched me, for I knew it when power went out of me." ⁴⁷ The woman saw that she had been found out, so she came, trembling, and threw herself at Jesus' feet. There, in front of everybody, she told him why she had touched him and how she had been healed at once. ⁴⁸ Jesus said to her, "My daughter, your faith has made you well. Go in peace."

⁴⁹ While Jesus was saying this, a messenger came from the official's house. "Your daughter has died," he told Jairus; "don't bother the Teacher any longer." ⁵⁰ But Jesus heard it and said to Jairus, "Don't be afraid; only believe, and she will be well." ⁵¹ When he arrived at the house he would not let anyone go in with him except Peter, John, and James, and the child's father and mother. ⁵² Everyone there was crying and mourning for the child. Jesus said, "Don't cry; the child is not dead — she is only sleeping!" ⁵³ They all made fun of him, because they knew that she was dead. ⁵⁴ But Jesus took her by the hand and called out, "Get up, child!" ⁵⁵ Her life returned and she got up at once; and Jesus ordered them to give her something to eat. ⁵⁶ Her parents were astounded, but Jesus commanded them not to tell anyone what had happened.

Jesus Sends out the Twelve Disciples
(Also Matt. 10.5–15; Mark 6.7–13)

9 Jesus called the twelve disciples together and gave them power and authority to drive out all demons and to cure diseases. ² Then he sent them out to preach the Kingdom of God and to heal the sick. ³ He said to them: "Take nothing with you for the journey: no walking stick, no beggar's bag, no food, no money, not even an extra shirt. ⁴ Wherever you are welcomed, stay in the same house until you leave that town; ⁵ wherever people don't welcome you, leave that town and shake the dust off your feet as a warning to them." ⁶ The disciples left and travelled through all the villages, preaching the Good News and healing people everywhere.

Herod's Confusion
(Also Matt. 14.1–12; Mark 6.14–29)

⁷ Herod, the ruler of Galilee, heard about all the things that were happening; he was very confused about it because some people said, "John the Baptist has come back to life!" ⁸ Others said that Elijah had appeared, while

others said that one of the prophets of long ago had come back to life. ⁹ Herod said, "I had John's head cut off; but who is this man I hear these things about?" And he kept trying to see Jesus.

Jesus Feeds the Five Thousand
(Also Matt. 14.13–21; Mark 6.30–44; John 6.1–14)

¹⁰ The apostles came back and told Jesus everything they had done. He took them with him and they went off by themselves to a town named Bethsaida. ¹¹ When the crowds heard about it they followed him. He welcomed them, spoke to them about the Kingdom of God, and healed those who needed it.

¹² When the sun had begun to set, the twelve disciples came to him and said, "Send the people away so they can go to the villages and farms around here and find food and lodging; for this is a lonely place." ¹³ But Jesus said to them, "You yourselves give them something to eat." They answered, "All we have is five loaves and two fish. Do you want us to go and buy food for this whole crowd?" ¹⁴ (There were about five thousand men there.) Jesus said to his disciples, "Make the people sit down in groups of about fifty each." ¹⁵ The disciples did so and made them all sit down. ¹⁶ Jesus took the five loaves and two fish, looked up to heaven, thanked God for them, broke them, and gave them to the disciples to distribute to the people. ¹⁷ They all ate and had enough; and the disciples took up twelve baskets of what the people left over.

Peter's Declaration about Jesus
(Also Matt. 16.13–19; Mark 8.27–29)

¹⁸ One time when Jesus was praying alone, the disciples came to him. "Who do the crowds say I am?" he asked them. ¹⁹ "Some say that you are John the Baptist," they answered. "Others say that you are Elijah, while others say that one of the prophets of long ago has come back to life." ²⁰ "What about you?" he asked them. "Who do you say I am?" Peter answered, "You are God's Messiah!"

Jesus Speaks about His Suffering and Death
(Also Matt. 16.20–28; Mark 8.30—9.1)

²¹ Then Jesus gave them strict orders not to tell this to anyone, ²² and added: "The Son of Man must suffer much,

and be rejected by the elders, the chief priests, and the teachers of the Law. He will be put to death, and be raised to life on the third day."

²³ And he said to all: "If anyone wants to come with me, he must forget himself, take up his cross every day, and follow me. ²⁴ For the person who wants to save his own life will lose it; but the one who loses his life for my sake will save it. ²⁵ Will a man gain anything if he wins the whole world but is himself lost or defeated? Of course not! ²⁶ If a man is ashamed of me and of my teaching, then the Son of Man will be ashamed of him when he comes in his glory and the glory of the Father and of the holy angels. ²⁷ Remember this! There are some here, I tell you, who will not die until they have seen the Kingdom of God."

The Transfiguration
(Also Matt. 17.1–8; Mark 9.2–8)

²⁸ About a week after he had said these things, Jesus took Peter, John, and James with him and went up a hill to pray. ²⁹ While he was praying, his face changed its appearance and his clothes became dazzling white. ³⁰ Suddenly two men were there talking with him. They were Moses and Elijah, ³¹ who appeared in heavenly glory and talked with Jesus about how he would soon fulfil God's purpose by dying in Jerusalem. ³² Peter and his companions were sound asleep, but they awoke and saw Jesus' glory and the two men who were standing with him. ³³ As the men were leaving Jesus, Peter said to him: "Master, it is a good thing that we are here. We will make three tents, one for you, one for Moses, and one for Elijah." (He really did not know what he was saying.) ³⁴ While he was still speaking, a cloud appeared and covered them with its shadow, and the disciples were afraid as the cloud came over them. ³⁵ A voice said from the cloud: "This is my Son, whom I have chosen — listen to him!" ³⁶ When the voice stopped, there was Jesus all alone. The disciples kept quiet about all this, and told no one at that time a single thing they had seen.

Jesus Heals a Boy with an Evil Spirit
(Also Matt. 17.14–18; Mark 9.14–27)

³⁷ The next day they went down from the hill, and a large crowd met Jesus. ³⁸ A man shouted from the crowd:

"Teacher! Look, I beg you, at my son — my only son!
[39] A spirit attacks him with a sudden shout and throws him
into a fit, so that he foams at the mouth; it keeps on hurt-
ing him and will hardly let him go! [40] I begged your
disciples to drive it out, but they could not." [41] Jesus
answered: "How unbelieving and wrong you people are!
How long must I stay with you? How long do I have to
put up with you?" Then he said to the man, "Bring your
son here." [42] As the boy was coming, the demon knocked
him to the ground and threw him into a fit. Jesus gave
a command to the evil spirit, healed the boy, and gave him
back to his father. [43] All the people were amazed at the
mighty power of God.

Jesus Speaks again about His Death
(Also Matt. 17.22–23; Mark 9.30–32)

The people were still marvelling at everything Jesus was
doing, when he said to his disciples: [44] "Don't forget what
I am about to tell you! The Son of Man is going to be
handed over to the power of men." [45] But they did not
know what this meant. It had been hidden from them so
that they could not understand it, and they were afraid
to ask him about the matter.

Who Is the Greatest?
(Also Matt. 18.1–5; Mark 9.33–37)

[46] An argument came up among the disciples as to which

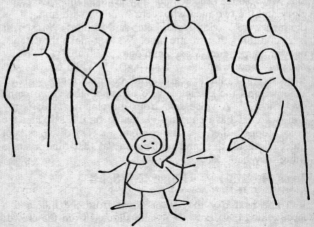

one of them was the greatest. [47] Jesus knew what they were thinking, so he took a child, stood him by his side, [48] and said to them: "The person who in my name welcomes this child, welcomes me; and whoever welcomes me, also welcomes the one who sent me. For he who is least among you all is the greatest."

Who Is not against You Is for You
(Also Mark 9.38–40)

[49] John spoke up. "Master," he said, "we saw a man driving out demons in your name, and we told him to stop, because he doesn't belong to our group." [50] "Do not try to stop him," Jesus said to him and to the other disciples; "for whoever is not against you is for you."

A Samaritan Village Refuses to Receive Jesus

[51] As the days drew near when Jesus would be taken up to heaven, he made up his mind and set out on his way to Jerusalem. [52] He sent messengers ahead of him, who left and went into a Samaritan village to get everything ready for him. [53] But the people there would not receive him, because it was plain that he was going to Jerusalem. [54] When the disciples James and John saw this they said, "Lord, do you want us to call fire down from heaven and destroy them?" [55] Jesus turned and rebuked them; [56] and they went on to another village.

The Would-Be Followers of Jesus
(Also Matt. 8.19–22)

[57] As they went on their way, a certain man said to Jesus, "I will follow you wherever you go." [58] Jesus said to him, "Foxes have holes, and birds have nests, but the Son of Man has no place to lie down and rest." [59] He said to another man, "Follow me." But he said, "Sir, first let me go and bury my father." [60] Jesus answered, "Let the dead bury their own dead. You go and preach the Kingdom of God." [61] Another man said, "I will follow you, sir; but first let me go and say good-bye to my family." [62] Jesus said to him, "Anyone who starts to plow and then keeps looking back is of no use for the Kingdom of God."

Jesus Sends out the Seventy-two

10 After this the Lord chose another seventy-two men and sent them out, two by two, to go ahead of him to every town and place where he himself was about to go. ² He said to them: "There is a great harvest, but few workers to gather it in. Pray to the owner of the harvest that he will send out more workers to gather in his harvest. ³ Go! I am sending you like lambs among wolves. ⁴ Don't take a purse, or a beggar's bag, or shoes; don't stop to greet anyone on the road. ⁵ Whenever you go into a house, first say, 'Peace be with this house.' ⁶ If a peace-loving man lives there, let your greeting of peace remain on him; if not, take back your greeting of peace. ⁷ Stay in that same house, eating and drinking what they offer you; for a worker should be given his pay. Don't move around from one house to another. ⁸ Whenever you go into a town and are made welcome, eat what is set before you, ⁹ heal the sick in that town, and say to the people there, 'The Kingdom of God has come near you.' ¹⁰ But whenever you go into a town and are not welcomed there, go out in the streets and say, ¹¹ 'Even the dust from your town that sticks to our feet we wipe off against you; but remember this, the Kingdom of God has come near you!' ¹² I tell you that on the Judgment Day God will show more mercy to Sodom than to that town!"

The Unbelieving Towns
(Also Matt. 11.20–24)

¹³ "How terrible it will be for you, Chorazin! How terrible for you too, Bethsaida! For if the miracles which were performed in you had been performed in Tyre and Sidon, long ago the people there would have sat down, put on sackcloth, and sprinkled ashes on themselves to show that they had turned from their sins! ¹⁴ God will show more mercy on the Judgment Day to Tyre and Sidon than to you. ¹⁵ And as for you, Capernaum! You wanted to lift yourself up to heaven? You will be thrown down to hell!"

¹⁶ He said to his disciples: "Whoever listens to you, listens to me; whoever rejects you, rejects me; and whoever rejects me, rejects the one who sent me."

The Return of the Seventy-two

¹⁷ The seventy-two men came back in great joy. "Lord," they said, "even the demons obeyed us when we commanded them in your name!" ¹⁸ Jesus answered them: "I saw Satan fall like lightning from heaven. ¹⁹ Listen! I have given you authority, so that you can walk on snakes and scorpions, and over all the power of the Enemy, and nothing will hurt you. ²⁰ But don't be glad because the evil spirits obey you; rather be glad because your names are written in heaven."

Jesus Rejoices
(Also Matt. 11.25–27; 13.16–17)

²¹ At that same time Jesus was filled with joy by the Holy Spirit, and said: "O Father, Lord of heaven and earth! I thank you because you have shown to the unlearned what you have hidden from the wise and learned. Yes, Father, this was done by your own choice and pleasure.
²² "My Father has given me all things: no one knows who the Son is except the Father, and no one knows who the Father is except the Son and those to whom the Son wants to reveal him."
²³ Then Jesus turned to the disciples and said to them privately: "How happy are you, to see the things you see! ²⁴ For many prophets and kings, I tell you, wanted to see what you see, but they could not, and to hear what you hear, but they did not."

The Parable of the Good Samaritan

²⁵ Then a certain teacher of the Law came up and tried to trap Jesus. "Teacher," he asked, "what must I do to receive eternal life?" ²⁶ Jesus answered him, "What do the Scriptures say? How do you interpret them?" ²⁷ The man answered: " 'You must love the Lord your God with all your heart, and with all your soul, and with all your strength, and with all your mind'; and, 'You must love your neighbour as yourself.' " ²⁸ "Your answer is correct," replied Jesus; "do this and you will live."
²⁹ But the teacher of the Law wanted to put himself in the right, so he asked Jesus, "Who is my neighbour?" ³⁰ Jesus answered: "A certain man was going down from

Jerusalem to Jericho, when robbers attacked him, stripped him and beat him up, leaving him half dead. ³¹ It so happened that a priest was going down that road; when he saw the man he walked on by, on the other side. ³² In the same way a Levite also came there, went over and looked at the man, and then walked on by, on the other side. ³³ But a certain Samaritan who was traveling that way came upon him, and when he saw the man his heart was filled with pity. ³⁴ He went over to him, poured oil and wine on his wounds and bandaged them; then he put the man on his own animal and took him to an inn, where he took care of him. ³⁵ The next day he took out two silver coins and gave them to the innkeeper. 'Take care of him,' he told the innkeeper, 'and when I come back this way I will pay you back whatever you spend on him.'" ³⁶ And Jesus concluded, "Which one of these three seems to you to have been a neighbour to the man attacked by the robbers?" ³⁷ The teacher of the Law answered, "The one who was kind to him." Jesus replied, "You go, then, and do the same."

Jesus Visits Martha and Mary

38 As Jesus and his disciples went on their way, he came to a certain village where a woman named Martha welcomed him in her home. 39 She had a sister named Mary, who sat down at the feet of the Lord and listened to his teaching. 40 Martha was upset over all the work she had to do; so she came and said, "Lord, don't you care that my sister has left me to do all the work by myself? Tell her to come and help me!" 41 The Lord answered her, "Martha, Martha! You are worried and troubled over so many things, 42 but just one is needed. Mary has chosen the right thing, and it will not be taken away from her."

Jesus' Teaching on Prayer
(Also Matt. 6.9–13; 7.7–11)

11 One time Jesus was praying in a certain place. When he finished, one of his disciples said to him, "Lord, teach us to pray, just as John taught his disciples." 2 Jesus said to them, "This is what you should pray:

'Father,
May your name be kept holy,
May your Kingdom come.
3 Give us day by day the food we need.
4 Forgive us our sins,
For we forgive everyone who has done us wrong.
And do not bring us to hard testing.' "

5 And Jesus said to his disciples: "Suppose one of you should go to a friend's house at midnight and tell him, 'Friend, let me borrow three loaves of bread. 6 A friend of mine who is on a journey has just come to my house and I don't have a thing to offer him!' 7 And suppose your friend should answer from inside, 'Don't bother me! The door is already locked, my children and I are in bed, and I can't get up to give you anything.' 8 Well, what then? I tell you, even if he will not get up and give you the bread because he is your friend, yet he will get up and give you everything you need because you are not ashamed to keep on asking. 9 And so I say to you: Ask, and you will receive; seek, and you will find; knock, and the door will be opened to you. 10 For everyone who asks will receive, and he who seeks will find, and the door will be opened to him who knocks. 11 Would any one of you fathers give his son

a snake when he asks for fish? ¹² Or would you give him a scorpion when he asks for an egg? ¹³ As bad as you are, you know how to give good things to your children. How much more, then, the Father in heaven will give the Holy Spirit to those who ask him!"

Jesus and Beelzebul
(Also Matt. 12.22–30; Mark 3.20–27)

¹⁴ Jesus was driving out a demon that could not talk; when the demon went out, the man began to talk. The crowds were amazed, ¹⁵ but some of them said, "It is Beelzebul, the chief of the demons, who gives him the power to drive them out." ¹⁶ Others wanted to trap him, so they asked him to perform a miracle to show God's approval. ¹⁷ But Jesus knew their thoughts and said to them: "Any country that divides itself into groups that fight one another will not last very long; a family divided against itself falls apart. ¹⁸ So if Satan's kingdom has groups fighting each other, how can it last? You say that I drive out demons because Beelzebul gives me the power to do so. ¹⁹ If this is how I drive them out, how do your followers drive them out? Your own followers prove that you are completely wrong! ²⁰ No, it is rather by means of God's power that I drive out demons, which proves that the Kingdom of God has already come to you.

²¹ "When a strong man, with all his weapons ready, guards his own house, all his belongings are safe. ²² But when a stronger man attacks him and defeats him, he carries away all the weapons the owner was depending on and divides up what he stole.

²³ "Anyone who is not for me, is really against me; anyone who does not help me gather, is really scattering."

The Return of the Evil Spirit
(Also Matt. 12.43–45)

²⁴ "When an evil spirit goes out of a man, it travels over dry country looking for a place to rest; if it doesn't find one, it says to itself, 'I will go back to my house which I left.' ²⁵ So it goes back and finds the house clean and all fixed up. ²⁶ Then it goes out and brings seven other spirits even worse than itself, and they come and live there. So that man is in worse shape, when it is all over, than he was at the beginning."

True Happiness

²⁷ When Jesus had said this, a woman spoke up from the crowd and said to him, "How happy is the woman who bore you and nursed you!" ²⁸ But Jesus answered, "Rather, how happy are those who hear the word of God and obey it!"

The Demand for a Miracle
(Also Matt. 12.38–42)

²⁹ As the people crowded around Jesus he went on to say: "How evil are the people of this day! They ask for a miracle as a sign of God's approval, but none will be given them except the miracle of Jonah. ³⁰ In the same way that the prophet Jonah was a sign for the people of Nineveh, so the Son of Man will be a sign for the people of this day. ³¹ On the Judgment Day the Queen from the South will stand up and accuse the people of today, because she travelled halfway round the world to listen to Solomon's wise teaching; and there is something here, I tell you, greater than Solomon. ³² On the Judgment Day the people of Nineveh will stand up and accuse you, because they turned from their sins when they heard Jonah preach; and there is something here, I tell you, greater than Jonah!"

The Light of the Body
(Also Matt. 5.15; 6.22–23)

³³ "No one lights a lamp and then hides it or puts it under a bowl; instead, he puts it on the lamp-stand, so that people may see the light as they come in. ³⁴ Your eyes are like a lamp for the body: when your eyes are clear your whole body is full of light; but when your eyes are bad your whole body will be in darkness. ³⁵ Be careful, then, that the light in you is not darkness. ³⁶ If, then, your whole body is full of light, with no part of it in darkness, it will be bright all over, as when a lamp shines on you with its brightness."

Jesus Accuses the Pharisees and the Teachers of the Law
(Also Matt. 23.1–36; Mark 12.38–40)

³⁷ When Jesus finished speaking, a Pharisee invited him

to eat with him; so he went in and sat down to eat. [38] The Pharisee was surprised when he noticed that Jesus had not washed before eating. [89] So the Lord said to him: "Now, then, you Pharisees clean the cup and plate on the outside, but inside you are full of violence and evil. [40] Fools! Did not God, who made the outside, also make the inside? [41] But give what is in your cups and plates to the poor, and everything will be clean for you.

[42] "How terrible for you, Pharisees! You give to God one tenth of the seasoning herbs, such as mint and rue and all the other herbs, but you neglect justice and the love for God. These you should practice, without neglecting the others.

[43] "How terrible for you, Pharisees! You love the reserved seats in the synagogues, and to be greeted with respect in the market places. [44] How terrible for you! You are like unmarked graves which people walk on without knowing it."

[45] One of the teachers of the Law said to him, "Teacher, when you say this you insult us too!" [46] Jesus answered: "How terrible for you, too, teachers of the Law!

You put loads on men's backs which are hard to carry, but you yourselves will not stretch out a finger to help them carry those loads. [47] How terrible for you! You make fine tombs for the prophets — the very prophets your ancestors murdered. [48] You yourselves admit, then, that you approve of what your ancestors did; for they murdered the prophets, and you build their tombs. [49] For this reason the Wisdom of God said: 'I will send them prophets and messengers; they will kill some of them and persecute others.' 50 So the people of this time will be punished for the murder of all the prophets killed since the creation of the world, 51 from the murder of Abel to the murder of Zechariah, who was killed between the altar and the holy place. Yes, I tell you, the people of this time will be punished for them all!

52 "How terrible for you, teachers of the Law! You have kept the key that opens the door to the house of knowledge; you yourselves will not go in, and you stop those who are trying to go in!"

53 When Jesus left that place the teachers of the Law and the Pharisees began to criticize him bitterly and ask him questions about many things, 54 trying to lay traps for him and catch him in something wrong he might say.

A Warning against Hypocrisy
(Also Matt. 10.26–27)

12 As thousands of people crowded together, so that they were stepping on each other, Jesus said first to his disciples: "Be on guard against the yeast of the Pharisees — I mean their hypocrisy. 2 Whatever is covered up will be uncovered, and every secret will be made known. 3 So then, whatever you have said in the dark will be heard in broad daylight, and whatever you have whispered in men's ears in a closed room will be shouted from the housetops."

Whom to Fear
(Also Matt. 10.28–31)

4 "I tell you, my friends, do not be afraid of those who kill the body but cannot afterwards do anything worse. 5 I will show you whom to fear: fear God who, after killing, has the authority to throw into hell. Yes, I tell you, be afraid of him!

6 "Aren't five sparrows sold for two pennies? Yet not a single one of them is forgotten by God. 7 Even the hairs of your head have all been numbered. So do not be afraid: you are worth much more than many sparrows!"

Confessing and Denying Christ
(Also Matt. 10.32–33; 12.32; 10.19–20)

8 "I tell you: whoever declares publicly that he belongs to me, the Son of Man will do the same for him before the

angels of God; [9] but whoever denies publicly that he belongs to me, the Son of Man will also deny him before the angels of God.

[10] "Anyone who says a word against the Son of Man will be forgiven; but the one who says evil things against the Holy Spirit will not be forgiven.

[11] "When they bring you to be tried in the synagogues, or before governors or rulers, do not be worried about how you will defend yourself or what you will say. [12] For the Holy Spirit will teach you at that time what you should say."

The Parable of the Rich Fool

[13] A man in the crowd said to him, "Teacher, tell my brother to divide with me the property our father left us." [14] Jesus answered him, "Man, who gave me the right to judge, or to divide the property between you two?" [15] And he went on to say to them all: "Watch out, and guard yourselves from all kinds of greed; for a man's true life is not made up of the things he owns, no matter how rich he may be." [16] Then Jesus told them this parable: "A rich man had land which bore good crops. [17] He began to think to himself, 'I don't have a place to keep all my crops. What can I do? [18] This is what I will do,' he told himself; 'I will tear my barns down and build bigger ones, where I will store the grain and all my other goods. [19] Then I will say to myself: Lucky man! You have all the good things you need for many years. Take life easy, eat, drink, and enjoy yourself!' [20] But God said to him, 'You fool! This very night you will have to give up your life; then who will get all these things you have kept for yourself?' " [21] And Jesus concluded, "This is how it is with those who pile up riches for themselves but are not rich in God's sight."

Trust in God
(Also Matt. 6.25–34)

[22] Then Jesus said to the disciples: "This is why I tell you: Do not be worried about the food you need to stay alive, or about the clothes you need for your body. [23] For life is much more important than food, and body much more important than clothes. [24] Look at the crows: they don't plant seeds or gather a harvest; they don't have stor-

age rooms or barns; God feeds them! You are worth so much more than birds! 25 Which one of you can live a few more years by worrying about it? 26 If you can't manage even such a small thing, why worry about the other things? 27 Look how the wild flowers grow: they don't work or make clothes for themselves. But I tell you that not even Solomon, as rich as he was, had clothes as beautiful as one of these flowers. 28 It is God who clothes the wild grass — grass that is here today, gone tomorrow, burned up in the oven. Won't he be all the more sure to clothe you? How little is your faith! 29 So don't be all upset, always looking for what you will eat and drink. 80 (For the heathen of this world are always looking for all these things.) Your Father knows that you need these things. 31 Instead, put his Kingdom first in your life, and he will provide you with these things."

Riches in Heaven
(Also Matt. 6.19–21)

32 "Do not be afraid, little flock! For your Father is pleased to give you the Kingdom. 33 Sell all your belongings and give the money to the poor. Provide for yourselves purses that don't wear out, and save your riches in heaven, where they will never decrease, for no thief can get to them, no moth can destroy them. 34 For your heart will always be where your riches are."

Watchful Servants

85 "Be ready for whatever comes, with your clothes fastened tight at the waist and your lamps lit, 86 like serv-

ants who are waiting for their master to come back from a wedding feast. When he comes and knocks, they will open the door for him at once. [37] How happy are those servants whose master finds them awake and ready! I tell you, he will fasten his belt, have them sit down, and wait on them. [38] How happy are they if he finds them ready, even if he should come as late as midnight or even later! [39] And remember this! If the man of the house knew the time when the thief would come, he would not let the thief break into his house. [40] And you, too, be ready, because the Son of Man will come at an hour when you are not expecting him."

The Faithful or the Unfaithful Servant
(Also Matt. 24.45-51)

[41] Peter said, "Lord, are you telling this parable to us, or do you mean it for everybody?" [42] The Lord answered: "Who, then, is the faithful and wise servant? He is the one whom his master will put in charge, to run the household and give the other servants their share of the food at the proper time. [43] How happy is that servant if his master finds him doing this when he comes home! [44] Indeed, I tell you, the master will put that servant in charge of all his property. [45] But if that servant says to himself, 'My master is taking a long time to come back,' and begins to beat the other servants, both men and women, and eats and drinks and gets drunk, [46] then the master will come back some day when the servant does not expect him and at a time he does not know; the master will cut him to pieces, and make him share the fate of the disobedient.

[47] "The servant who knows what his master wants him to do, but does not get himself ready and do what his master wants, will be punished with a heavy whipping; [48] but the servant who does not know what his master wants, and does something for which he deserves a whipping, will be punished with a light whipping. The man to whom much is given, of him much is required; the man to whom more is given, of him much more is required."

Jesus the Cause of Division
(Also Matt. 10.34-36)

[49] "I came to set the earth on fire, and how I wish it were already kindled! [50] I have a baptism to receive, and

how distressed I am until it is over! [51] Do you suppose that I came to bring peace to the world? Not peace, I tell you, but division. [52] From now on a family of five will be divided, three against two, two against three. [53] Fathers will be against their sons, and sons against their fathers; mothers will be against their daughters, and daughters against their mothers; mothers-in-law will be against their daughters-in-law, and daughters-in-law against their mothers-in-law."

Understanding the Time
(Also Matt. 16.2–3)

[54] Jesus said also to the people: "When you see a cloud coming up in the west, at once you say, 'It is going to rain,' and it does. [55] And when you feel the south wind blowing, you say, 'It is going to get hot,' and it does. [56] Impostors! You can look at the earth and the sky and tell what it means; why, then, don't you know the meaning of this present time?"

Settle with Your Opponent
(Also Matt. 5.25–26)

[57] "And why do you not judge for yourselves the right thing to do? [58] If a man brings a lawsuit against you and takes you to court, do your best to settle the matter with him while you are on the way, so that he won't drag you before the judge, and the judge hand you over to the police, and the police put you in jail. [59] You will not come out of there, I tell you, until you pay the last penny of your fine."

Turn from Your Sins or Die

13 At that time some people were there who told Jesus about the Galileans whom Pilate had killed while they were offering sacrifices to God. [2] Jesus answered them: "Because these Galileans were killed in that way, do you think it proves that they were worse sinners than all the other Galileans? [3] No! I tell you that if you do not turn from your sins, you will all die as they did. [4] What about those eighteen in Siloam who were killed when the tower fell on them? Do you suppose this proves that they were worse than all the other people living in Jerusalem? [5] No!

I tell you that if you do not turn from your sins, you will all die as they did."

The Parable of the Unfruitful Fig Tree

⁶ Then Jesus told them this parable: "A man had a fig tree growing in his vineyard. He went looking for figs on it but found none. ⁷ So he said to his gardener, 'Look, for three years I have been coming here looking for figs on this fig tree and I haven't found any. Cut it down! Why should it go on using up the soil?' ⁸ But the gardener answered, 'Leave it alone, sir, just this one year; I will dig a trench round it and fill it up with fertilizer. ⁹ Then if the tree bears figs next year, so much the better; if not, then you will have it cut down.' "

Jesus Heals a Crippled Woman on the Sabbath

¹⁰ One Sabbath day Jesus was teaching in a synagogue. ¹¹ A woman was there who had an evil spirit in her that had kept her sick for eighteen years; she was bent over and could not straighten up at all. ¹² When Jesus saw her he called out to her, "Woman, you are free from your sickness!" ¹³ He placed his hands on her and at once she straightened herself up and praised God. ¹⁴ The official of the synagogue was angry that Jesus had healed on the Sabbath; so he spoke up and said to the people, "There are six days in which we should work; so come during those days and be healed, but not on the Sabbath!" ¹⁵ The Lord answered him by saying: "You impostors! Any one of you would untie his ox or his donkey from the stall and take it out to give it water on the Sabbath. ¹⁶ Now here is this

descendant of Abraham whom Satan has kept in bonds for eighteen years; should she not be freed from her bonds on the Sabbath?" ¹⁷ His answer made all his enemies ashamed of themselves, while all the people rejoiced over every wonderful thing that he did.

The Parable of the Mustard Seed
(Also Matt. 13.31–32; Mark 4.30–32)

¹⁸ Jesus said: "What is the Kingdom of God like? What can I compare it with? ¹⁹ It is like a mustard seed, which a man took and planted in his field; the plant grew and became a tree, and the birds made their nests in its branches."

The Parable of the Yeast
(Also Matt. 13.33)

²⁰ Again Jesus asked: "What shall I compare the Kingdom of God with? ²¹ It is like the yeast which a woman takes and mixes in a bushel of flour, until the whole batch of dough rises."

The Narrow Door
(Also Matt. 7.13–14, 21–23)

²² Jesus went through towns and villages, teaching and making his way towards Jerusalem. ²³ Someone asked him, "Sir, will just a few people be saved?" Jesus answered them: ²⁴ "Do your best to go in through the narrow door; for many people, I tell you, will try to go in but will not be able.

²⁵ "The master of the house will get up and close the door; then when you stand outside and begin to knock on the door and say, 'Open the door for us, sir!' he will answer you, 'I don't know where you come from!' ²⁶ Then you will answer back, 'We ate and drank with you; you taught in our town!' ²⁷ He will say again, 'I don't know where you come from. Get away from me, all you evil-doers!' ²⁸ What crying and gnashing of teeth there will be when you see Abraham, Isaac, and Jacob and all the prophets in the Kingdom of God, while you are kept outside! ²⁹ People will come from the east and the west, from the north and the south, and sit at the table in the Kingdom of God. ³⁰ Then those who are now last will be first, and those who are now first will be last."

Jesus' Love for Jerusalem
(Also Matt. 23.37-39)

[31] At that same time some Pharisees came to Jesus and said to him, "You must get out of here and go somewhere else, for Herod wants to kill you." [32] Jesus answered them: "Go tell that fox: 'I am driving out demons and performing cures today and tomorrow, and on the third day I shall finish my work.' [33] Yet I must be on my way today, tomorrow, and the next day; it is not right for a prophet to be killed anywhere except in Jerusalem.

[34] "O Jerusalem, Jerusalem! You kill the prophets, you stone the messengers God has sent you! How many times I wanted to put my arms round all your people, just as a hen gathers her chicks under her wings, but you would not let me! [35] Now your home will be completely forsaken. You will not see me, I tell you, until the time comes when you say, 'God bless him who comes in the name of the Lord.' "

Jesus Heals a Sick Man

14 One Sabbath day Jesus went to eat a meal at the home of one of the leading Pharisees; and people were watching Jesus closely. [2] A man whose legs and arms were swollen came to Jesus, [3] and Jesus spoke up and asked the teachers of the Law and the Pharisees, "Does our Law allow healing on the Sabbath, or not?" [4] But they would not say a thing. Jesus took the man, healed him and sent him away. [5] Then he said to them, "If any one of you had a son or an ox that happened to fall in a well on a Sabbath, would you not pull him out at once on the Sabbath itself?" [6] But they were not able to answer him about this.

Hospitality and Humility

[7] Jesus noticed how some of the guests were choosing the best places, so he told this parable to all of them: [8] "When someone invites you to a wedding feast, do not sit down in the best place. For it could happen that someone more important than you had been invited, [9] and your host, who invited both of you, would come and say to you, 'Let him have this place.' Then you would be ashamed and have to sit in the lowest place. [10] Instead, when you are invited, go and sit in the lowest place, so that your host

will come to you and say, 'Come on up, my friend, to a better place.' This will bring you honour in the presence of all the other guests. ¹¹ For everyone who makes himself great will be humbled, and whoever humbles himself will be made great."

¹² Then Jesus said to his host: "When you give a lunch or a dinner, do not invite your friends, or your brothers, or your relatives, or your rich neighbours — for they will invite you back and in this way you will be paid for what you did. ¹³ When you give a feast, invite the poor, the crippled, the lame, and the blind, ¹⁴ and you will be blessed; for they are not able to pay you back. You will be paid by God when the good people are raised from death."

The Parable of the Great Feast
(Also Matt. 22.1–10)

¹⁵ One of the men sitting at the table heard this and said to Jesus, "How happy are those who will sit at the table in the Kingdom of God!" ¹⁶ Jesus said to him: "There was a man who was giving a great feast, to which he invited many people. ¹⁷ At the time for the feast he sent his servant to tell his guests, 'Come, everything is ready!' ¹⁸ But they all began, one after another, to make excuses. The first one told the servant, 'I bought a field, and have to go and look at it; please accept my apologies.' ¹⁹ Another one said, 'I bought five pairs of oxen and am on my way to try them out; please accept my apologies.' ²⁰ Another one said, 'I have just got married, and for this reason I cannot come.' ²¹ The servant went back and told all this to his master. The master of the house was furious and said to his servant, 'Hurry out to the streets and alleys of the town, and bring back the poor, the crippled, the blind, and the lame.' ²² Soon the servant said, 'Your order has been carried out, sir, but there is room for more.' ²³ So the master said to the servant, 'Go out to the country roads and lanes, and make people come in, so that my house will be full. ²⁴ None of those men who were invited, I tell you all, will taste my dinner!' "

The Cost of Being a Disciple
(Also Matt. 10.37–38)

²⁵ Great crowds of people were going along with Jesus.

He turned and said to them: ²⁶ "Whoever comes to me cannot be my disciple unless he hates his father and his mother, his wife and his children, his brothers and his sisters, and himself as well. ²⁷ Whoever does not carry his own cross and come after me cannot be my disciple. ²⁸ If one of you is planning to build a tower, he sits down first and figures out what it will cost, to see if he has enough money to finish the job. ²⁹ If he doesn't, he will not be able to finish the tower after laying the foundation; and all who see what happened will make fun of him. ³⁰ 'This man began to build but can't finish the job!' they will say. ³¹ If a king goes out with ten thousand men to fight another king, who comes against him with twenty thousand men, he will sit down first and decide if he is strong enough to face that other king. ³² If he isn't, he will have to send messengers to meet the other king, while he is still a long way off, to ask for terms of peace. ³³ In the same way," concluded Jesus, "none of you can be my disciple unless he gives up everything he has."

Worthless Salt
(Also Matt. 5.13; Mark 9.50)

³⁴ "Salt is good, but if it loses its taste there is no way to make it good again. ³⁵ It is no good for the soil or for the manure pile; it is thrown away. Listen, then, if you have ears!"

The Lost Sheep
(Also Matt. 18.12–14)

15 One time many tax collectors and outcasts came to listen to Jesus. ² The Pharisees and the teachers of the Law started grumbling, "This man welcomes outcasts and even eats with them!" ³ So Jesus told them this parable:
⁴ "Suppose one of you has a hundred sheep and loses one of them — what does he do? He leaves the ninety-nine sheep in the pasture and goes looking for the lost sheep until he finds it. ⁵ When he finds it, he is so happy that he puts it on his shoulders, ⁶ carries it back home, and calls his friends and neighbours together. 'Rejoice with me,' he tells them, 'for I have found my lost sheep!' ⁷ In the same way, I tell you, there will be more joy in heaven over one sinner who repents than over ninety-nine respectable people who do not need to repent."

The Lost Coin

8 "Or suppose a woman who has ten silver coins loses one of them — what does she do? She lights a lamp, sweeps her house, and looks carefully everywhere until she finds it. 9 When she finds it, she calls her friends and neighbours together. 'Rejoice with me,' she tells them, 'for I have found the coin I lost!' 10 In the same way, I tell you, the angels of God rejoice over one sinner who repents."

The Lost Son

11 Jesus went on to say: "There was a man who had two sons. 12 The younger one said to his father, 'Father, give me now my share of the property.' So the father divided the property between his two sons. 13 After a few days the younger son sold his part of the property and left home

with the money. He went to a country far away, where he wasted his money in reckless living. 14 He spent everything he had. Then a severe famine spread over that country, and he was left without a thing. 15 So he went to work for one of the citizens of that country, who sent him out to his farm to take care of the pigs. 16 He wished he could fill himself with the bean pods the pigs ate, but no one gave him any. 17 At last he came to his senses and said: 'All my father's hired workers have more than they can eat, and here I am, about to starve! 18 I will get up and go to my father and say, "Father, I have sinned against God and against you. 19 I am no longer fit to be called your son; treat me as one of your hired workers." ' 20 So he got up and started back to his father.

"He was still a long way from home when his father saw him; his heart was filled with pity and he ran, threw his arms round his son, and kissed him. [21] 'Father,' the son said, 'I have sinned against God and against you. I am no longer fit to be called your son.' [22] But the father called his servants: 'Hurry!' he said. 'Bring the best robe and put it on him. Put a ring on his finger and shoes on his feet. [23] Then go get the prize calf and kill it, and let us celebrate with a feast! [24] For this son of mine was dead,

but now he is alive; he was lost, but now he has been found.' And so the feasting began.

[25] "The older son, in the meantime, was out in the field. On his way back, when he came close to the house, he heard the music and dancing. [26] He called one of the serv-

ants and asked him, 'What's going on?' 27 'Your brother came back home,' the servant answered, 'and your father killed the prize calf, because he got him back safe and sound.' 28 The older brother was so angry that he would not go into the house; so his father came out and begged him to come in. 29 'Look,' he answered back to his father, 'all these years I have worked like a slave for you, and not once did I disobey an order of yours. What have you given me? Not even a goat for me to have a feast with my friends! 30 But this son of yours wasted all your property on prostitutes, and when he comes back home you kill the prize calf for him!' 31 'My son,' the father answered, 'you are always at home and everything I have is yours. 32 But we had to have a feast and be happy, for your brother was dead, but now he is alive; he was lost, but now he has been found.' "

The Shrewd Manager

16 Jesus said to his disciples: "There was a rich man who had a manager, and he was told that the manager was wasting his master's money. 2 He called him in and said, 'What is this I hear about you? Turn in a complete account of your handling of my property, for you cannot be my manager any longer.' 3 'My master is about to dismiss me from my job,' the man said to himself. 'What shall I do? I am not strong enough to dig ditches, and I am ashamed to beg. 4 Now I know what I will do! Then when my job is gone I shall have friends who will welcome me in their homes.' 5 So he called in all the people who were in debt to his master. To the first one he said, 'How much do you owe my master?' 6 'One hundred barrels of olive oil,' he answered. 'Here is your account,' the manager told him; 'sit down and write fifty.' 7 To another one he said, 'And you — how much do you owe?' 'A thousand bushels of wheat,' he answered. 'Here is your account,' the manager told him; 'write eight hundred.' 8 The master of this dishonest manager praised him for doing such a shrewd thing; for the people of this world are much more shrewd in handling their affairs than the people who belong to the light."

9 And Jesus went on to say: "And so I tell you: make friends for yourselves with worldly wealth, so that when it gives out you will be welcomed in the eternal home.

¹⁰ Whoever is faithful in small matters will be faithful in large ones; whoever is dishonest in small matters will be dishonest in large ones. ¹¹ If, then, you have not been faithful in handling worldly wealth, how can you be trusted with true wealth? ¹² And if you have not been faithful in what belongs to someone else, who will give you what belongs to you?

¹³ "No servant can be the slave of two masters: he will hate one and love the other; he will be loyal to one and despise the other. You cannot serve both God and money."

Some Sayings of Jesus
(Also Matt. 11.12–13; 5.31–32; Mark 10.11–12)

¹⁴ The Pharisees heard all this, and they made fun of Jesus, because they loved money. ¹⁵ Jesus said to them: "You are the ones who make yourselves look right in men's sight, but God knows your hearts. For what men think is of great value is worth nothing in God's sight.

¹⁶ "The Law of Moses and the writings of the prophets were in effect up to the time of John the Baptist; since then the Good News about the Kingdom of God is being told, and everyone forces his way in. ¹⁷ But it is easier for heaven and earth to disappear than for the smallest detail of the Law to be done away with.

¹⁸ "Any man who divorces his wife and marries another woman commits adultery; and the man who marries a divorced woman commits adultery."

The Rich Man and Lazarus

¹⁹ "There was once a rich man who dressed in the most expensive clothes and lived in great luxury every day. ²⁰ There was also a poor man, named Lazarus, full of sores, who used to be brought to the rich man's door, ²¹ hoping to fill himself with the bits of food that fell from the rich man's table. Even the dogs would come and lick his sores. ²² The poor man died and was carried by the angels to Abraham's side, at the feast in heaven; the rich man died and was buried. ²³ He was in great pain in Hades; and he looked up and saw Abraham, far away, with Lazarus at his side. ²⁴ So he called out, 'Father Abraham! Take pity on me, and send Lazarus to dip his finger in some water and cool off my tongue, for I am in great pain in

this fire!' ²⁵ But Abraham said: 'Remember, my son, that in your lifetime you were given all the good things, while Lazarus got all the bad things; but now he is enjoying it here, while you are in pain. ²⁶ Besides all that, there is a deep pit lying between us, so that those who want to cross over from here to you cannot do it, nor can anyone cross over to us from where you are.' ²⁷ The rich man said, 'Well, father, I beg you, send Lazarus to my father's house, ²⁸ where I have five brothers; let him go and warn them so that they, at least, will not come to this place of pain.' ²⁹ Abraham said, 'Your brothers have Moses and the prophets to warn them; let your brothers listen to what they say.' ³⁰ The rich man answered, 'That is not enough, father Abraham! But if someone were to rise from death and go to them, then they would turn from their sins.' ³¹ But Abraham said, 'If they will not listen to Moses and the prophets, they will not be convinced even if someone were to rise from death.' "

Sin
(*Also Matt. 18.6–7, 21–22; Mark 9.42*)

17 Jesus said to his disciples: "Things that make people fall into sin are bound to happen; but how terrible for the one who makes them happen! ² It would be better for him if a large millstone were tied around his neck and he were thrown into the sea, than for him to cause one of these little ones to sin. ³ Be on your guard!

"If your brother sins, rebuke him, and if he repents, forgive him. ⁴ If he sins against you seven times in one day, and each time he comes to you saying, 'I repent,' you must forgive him."

Faith

⁵ The apostles said to the Lord, "Make our faith greater." ⁶ The Lord answered: "If you had faith as big as a mustard seed, you could say to this mulberry tree, 'Pull yourself up by the roots and plant yourself in the sea!' and it would obey you."

A Servant's Duty

⁷ "Suppose one of you has a servant who is ploughing or looking after the sheep. When he comes in from the field, do you say to him, 'Hurry along and eat your meal'?

⁸ Of course not! Instead, you say to him, 'Get my supper ready, then put on your apron and wait on me while I eat and drink; after that you may eat and drink.' ⁹ The servant does not deserve thanks for obeying orders, does he? ¹⁰ It is the same with you; when you have done all you have been told to do, say, 'We are ordinary servants; we have only done our duty.' "

Jesus Makes Ten Lepers Clean

¹¹ As Jesus made his way to Jerusalem he went between Samaria and Galilee. ¹² He was going into a certain village when he was met by ten lepers. They stood at a distance ¹³ and shouted, "Jesus! Master! Have pity on us!" ¹⁴ Jesus saw them and said to them, "Go and let the priests examine you." On the way they were made clean. ¹⁵ One of them, when he saw that he was healed, came back, praising God with a loud voice. ¹⁶ He threw himself to the ground at Jesus' feet, thanking him. The man was a Samaritan. ¹⁷ Jesus spoke up: "There were ten men made clean; where are the other nine? ¹⁸ Why is this foreigner the only one who came back to give thanks to God?" ¹⁹ And Jesus said to him, "Get up and go; your faith has made you well."

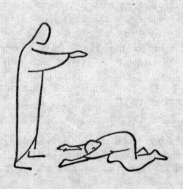

The Coming of the Kingdom
Also Matt. 24.23–28, 37–41)

20 Some Pharisees asked Jesus when the Kingdom of God would come. His answer was: "The Kingdom of God does not come in such a way as to be seen. 21 No one will say, 'Look, here it is!' or, 'There it is!'; because the Kingdom of God is within you."

22 Then he said to the disciples: "The time will come when you will wish you could see one of the days of the Son of Man, but you will not see it. 23 There will be those who will say to you, 'Look, over there!' or, 'Look, over here!' But don't go out looking for it. 24 As the lightning flashes across the sky and lights it up from one side to the other, so will the Son of Man be in his day. 25 But first he must suffer much and be rejected by the people of this day. 26 As it was in the time of Noah, so shall it be in the days of the Son of Man. 27 Everybody kept on eating and drinking, men and women married, up to the very day Noah went into the ark and the Flood came and killed them all. 28 It will be as it was in the time of Lot. Everybody kept on eating and drinking, buying and selling, planting and building. 29 On the day Lot left Sodom, fire and sulphur rained down from heaven and killed them all. 30 That is how it will be on the day the Son of Man is revealed.

31 "The man who is on the roof of his house on that day must not go down into his house to get his belongings that are there; in the same way, the man who is out in the field must not go back to the house. 32 Remember Lot's wife! 33 Whoever tries to save his own life will lose it; whoever loses his life will save it. 34 On that night, I tell you, there will be two men sleeping in one bed: one will be taken away, the other left behind. 35 Two women will be grinding meal together: one will be taken away, the other left behind. [36 Two men will be in the field: one will be taken away, the other left behind.]" 37 The disciples asked him, "Where, Lord?" Jesus answered, "Where there is a dead body the vultures will gather."

The Parable of the Widow and the Judge

18 Then Jesus told them this parable, to teach them that they should always pray and never become discouraged. 2 "There was a judge in a certain town who

neither feared God nor respected men. [8] And there was a widow in that same town who kept coming to him and pleading for her rights: 'Help me against my opponent! [4] For a long time the judge was not willing, but at last he said to himself, 'Even though I don't fear God or respect men, [5] yet because of all the trouble this widow is giving me I will see to it that she gets her rights; or else she will keep on coming and finally wear me out!' " [6] And the Lord continued: "Listen to what that corrupt judge said. [7] Now, will God not judge in favour of his own people who cry to him for help day and night? Will he be slow to help them? [8] I tell you, he will judge in their favour, and do it quickly. But will the Son of Man find faith on earth when he comes?"

The Parable of the Pharisee and the Tax Collector

[9] Jesus also told this parable to people who were sure of their own goodness and despised everybody else. [10] "Two men went up to the Temple to pray; one was a Pharisee, the other a tax collector. [11] The Pharisee stood apart by himself and prayed: 'I thank you, God, that I am not greedy, dishonest, or immoral, like everybody else; I thank you that I am not like that tax collector. [12] I fast two days every week, and I give you one tenth of all my income. [13] But the tax collector stood at a distance and would not even raise his face to heaven, but beat on his breast and said, 'O God, have pity on me, a sinner!' [14] I tell you," said Jesus, "this man, and not the other, was in the right with God when he went home. For everyone who makes himself great will be humbled, and everyone who humbles himself will be made great."

Jesus Blesses Little Children
(Also Matt. 19.13–15; Mark 10.13–16)

[15] Some people brought their babies to Jesus to have him place his hands on them. But the disciples saw them and scolded them for doing so. [16] But Jesus called the children to him, and said: "Let the children come to me! Do not stop them, because the Kingdom of God belongs to such as these. [17] Remember this! Whoever does not receive the Kingdom of God like a child will never enter it."

The Rich Man
(Also Matt. 19.16–30; Mark 10.17–31)

18 A certain Jewish leader asked him: "Good Teacher, what must I do to receive eternal life?" 19 "Why do you call me good?" Jesus asked him. "No one is good except God alone. 20 You know the commandments: 'Do not commit adultery; do not murder; do not steal; do not lie; honour your father and mother.' " 21 The man replied, "Ever since I was young I have obeyed all these commandments." 22 When Jesus heard this, he said to him: "You still need to do one thing. Sell all you have and give the money to the poor, and you will have riches in heaven; then come and follow me." 23 But when the man heard this he became very sad, because he was very rich.

24 Jesus saw that he was sad and said: "How hard it is for rich people to enter the Kingdom of God! 25 It is much harder for a rich man to enter the Kingdom of God than for a camel to go through the eye of a needle." 26 The people who heard him asked, "Who, then, can be saved?" 27 Jesus answered, "What is impossible for men is possible for God."

28 Then Peter said, "Look! We have left our homes to follow you." 29 "Yes," Jesus said to them, "and I tell you this: anyone who leaves home or wife or brothers or parents or children for the sake of the Kingdom of God 30 will receive much more in the present age, and eternal life in the age to come."

Jesus Speaks a Third Time about His Death
(Also Matt. 20.17–19; Mark 10.32–34)

31 Jesus took the twelve disciples aside and said to them: "Listen! We are going to Jerusalem where everything the prophets wrote about the Son of Man will come true. 32 He will be handed over to the Gentiles, who will make fun of him, insult him, and spit on him. 33 They will whip him and kill him, but on the third day he will be raised to life." 34 The disciples did not understand any of these things; the meaning of the words was hidden from them, and they did not know what Jesus was talking about.

Jesus Heals a Blind Beggar
(Also Matt. 20.29–34; Mark 10.46–52)

35 Jesus was coming near Jericho, and a certain blind

man was sitting and begging by the road. ³⁶ When he heard the crowd passing by he asked, "What is this?" ³⁷ "Jesus of Nazareth is passing by," they told him. ³⁸ He cried out, "Jesus! Son of David! Have mercy on me!" ³⁹ The people in front scolded him and told him to be quiet. But he shouted even more loudly, "Son of David! Have mercy on me!" ⁴⁰ So Jesus stopped and ordered that the blind man be brought to him. When he came near Jesus asked him, ⁴¹ "What do you want me to do for you?" "Sir," he answered, "I want to see again." ⁴² Then Jesus said to him, "See! Your faith has made you well." ⁴³ At once he was able to see, and he followed Jesus, giving thanks to God. When the crowd saw it, they all praised God.

Jesus and Zacchaeus

19 Jesus went on into Jericho and was passing through. ² There was a chief tax collector there, named Zacchaeus, who was rich. ³ He was trying to see who Jesus was, but he was a little man and could not see Jesus because of the crowd. ⁴ So he ran ahead of the crowd and climbed a sycamore tree to see Jesus, who would be going

that way. ⁵ When Jesus came to that place he looked up and said to Zacchaeus, "Hurry down, Zacchaeus, for I must stay in your house today." ⁶ Zacchaeus hurried down and welcomed him with great joy. ⁷ All the people who saw it started grumbling, "This man has gone as a guest to the home of a sinner!" ⁸ Zacchaeus stood up and said to the Lord, "Listen, sir! I will give half my belongings to the poor; and if I have cheated anyone, I will pay him back four times as much." ⁹ Jesus said to him, "Salvation has come to this house today; this man, also, is a descendant of Abraham. ¹⁰ For the Son of Man came to seek and to save the lost."

The Parable of the Gold Coins
(Also Matt. 25.14–30)

¹¹ Then Jesus told a parable to those who heard him say this. He was now almost at Jerusalem, and they supposed that the Kingdom of God was just about to appear. ¹² So he said: "There was a nobleman who went to a country far away to be made king and then come back home. ¹³ Before he left, he called his ten servants and gave them each a gold coin and told them, 'See what you can earn with this while I am gone.' ¹⁴ Now, his countrymen hated him, and so they sent messengers after him to say, 'We don't want this man to be our king.'

¹⁵ "The nobleman was made king and came back. At once he ordered his servants, to whom he had given the money, to appear before him in order to find out how much they had earned. ¹⁶ The first one came up and said, 'Sir, I have earned ten gold coins with the one you gave me.' ¹⁷ 'Well done,' he said; 'you are a good servant! Since you were faithful in small matters, I will put you in charge of ten cities.' ¹⁸ The second servant came and said, 'Sir, I have earned five gold coins with the one you gave me.' ¹⁹ To this one he said, 'You will be in charge of five cities.' ²⁰ Another servant came and said: 'Sir, here is your gold coin; I kept it hidden in a handkerchief. ²¹ I was afraid of you, because you are a hard man. You take what is not yours, and reap what you did not plant.' ²² He said to him: 'You bad servant! I will use your own words to condemn you! You know that I am a hard man, taking what is not mine and reaping what I have not planted. ²³ Well, then, why didn't you put my money in the bank? Then I would

have received it back with interest when I returned.'
²⁴ Then he said to those who were standing there, 'Take the
gold coin away from him and give it to the servant who
has ten coins.' ²⁵ They said to him, 'Sir, he already has
ten coins!' ²⁶ 'I tell you,' he replied, 'that to every one who
has, even more will be given; but the one who does not
have, even the little that he has will be taken away from
him. ²⁷ Now, as for these enemies of mine who did not
want me to be their king: bring them here and kill them
before me!' "

The Triumphant Entry into Jerusalem
(*Also Matt. 21.1–11; Mark 11.1–11; John 12.12–19*)

²⁸ Jesus said this and then went on to Jerusalem ahead
of them. ²⁹ As he came near Bethphage and Bethany, at
the Mount of Olives, he sent two disciples ahead ³⁰ with
these instructions: "Go to the village there ahead of you;
as you go in you will find a colt tied up that has never been
ridden. Untie it and bring it here. ³¹ If someone asks you,
'Why are you untying it?' tell him, 'The Master needs it.' "
³² They went on their way and found everything just as
Jesus had told them. ³³ As they were untying the colt, its
owners said to them, "Why are you untying it?" ³⁴ "The
Master needs it," they answered, ³⁵ and took the colt to

Jesus. Then they threw their cloaks over the animal and helped Jesus get on. ³⁶ As he rode on, they spread their cloaks on the road. ³⁷ When he came near Jerusalem, at the place where the road went down the Mount of Olives, the large crowd of his disciples began to thank God and praise him in loud voices for all the great things that they had seen: ³⁸ "God bless the king who comes in the name of the Lord! Peace in heaven, and glory to God!"

[39] Then some of the Pharisees spoke up from the crowd to Jesus. "Teacher," they said, "command your disciples to be quiet!" [40] Jesus answered, "If they keep quiet, I tell you, the stones themselves will shout."

Jesus Weeps over Jerusalem

[41] He came closer to the city and when he saw it he wept over it, [42] saying: "If you only knew today what is needed for peace! But now you cannot see it! [43] For the days will come upon you when your enemies will surround you with barricades, blockade you, and close in on you from every side. [44] They will completely destroy you and the people within your walls; not a single stone will they leave in its place, because you did not recognize the time when God came to save you!"

Jesus Goes to the Temple
(Also Matt. 21.12–17; Mark 11.15–19; John 2.13–22)

[45] Jesus went into the Temple and began to drive out the merchants, [46] saying to them: "It is written in the Scriptures that God said, 'My house will be called a house of prayer.' But you have turned it into a hideout for thieves!"

[47] Jesus taught in the Temple every day. The chief priests, the teachers of the Law, and the leaders of the people wanted to kill him, [48] but they could not find how to do it, because all the people kept listening to him, not wanting to miss a single word.

The Question about Jesus' Authority
(Also Matt. 21.23–27; Mark 11.27–33)

20 One day, when Jesus was in the Temple teaching the people and preaching the Good News, the chief priests and the teachers of the Law, together with the elders, came [2] and said to him, "Tell us, what right do you have to do these things? Who gave you the right to do them?" [3] Jesus answered them: "Now let me ask you a question. Tell me, [4] did John's right to baptize come from God or from man?" [5] They started to argue among themselves: "What shall we say? If we say, 'From God,' he will say, 'Why, then, did you not believe John?' [6] But if we say, 'From man,' this whole crowd here will stone us, because they are convinced that John was a prophet." [7] So

they answered, "We don't know where it came from."
⁸ And Jesus said to them, "Neither will I tell you, then, by
what right I do these things."

The Parable of the Tenants in the Vineyard
(Also Matt. 21.33–46; Mark 12.1–12)

⁹ Then Jesus told the people this parable: "A man
planted a vineyard, rented it out to tenants, and then left
home for a long time. ¹⁰ When the time came for harvest-
ing the grapes, he sent a slave to the tenants to receive
from them his share of the harvest. But the tenants beat
the slave and sent him back without a thing. ¹¹ So he sent
another slave, but the tenants beat him also, treated him
shamefully, and sent him back without a thing. ¹² Then he
sent a third slave; the tenants hurt him, too, and threw him
out. ¹³ Then the owner of the vineyard said, 'What shall
I do? I will send my own dear son; surely they will respect
him!' ¹⁴ But when the tenants saw him they said to one
another, 'This is the owner's son. Let us kill him, and the
vineyard will be ours!' ¹⁵ So they threw him out of the
vineyard and killed him.

"What, then, will the owner of the vineyard do to the
tenants?" Jesus asked. ¹⁶ "He will come and kill those men,
and turn over the vineyard to other tenants." When the
people heard this they said, "Surely not!" ¹⁷ Jesus looked
at them and asked, "What, then, does this scripture mean?

'The stone which the builders rejected as
    worthless
Turned out to be the most important stone.'

¹⁸ Everyone who falls on that stone will be cut to pieces;
and if the stone falls on someone, it will crush him to
dust."

The Question about Paying Taxes
(Also Matt. 22.15–22; Mark 12.13–17)

¹⁹ The teachers of the Law and the chief priests tried to
arrest Jesus on the spot, because they knew that he had
told this parable against them; but they were afraid of the
people. ²⁰ So they watched for the right time. They bribed
some men to pretend they were sincere, and sent them to
trap Jesus with questions, so they could hand him over to
the authority and power of the Governor. ²¹ These spies
said to Jesus: "Teacher, we know that what you say and

teach is right. We know that you pay no attention to what
a man seems to be, but teach the truth about God's will
for man. ²² Tell us, is it against our Law for us to pay
taxes to the Roman Emperor, or not?" ²³ But Jesus saw
through their trick and said to them, ²⁴ "Show me a silver
coin. Whose face and name are these on it?" "The Emperor's," they answered. ²⁵ So Jesus said, "Well, then, pay
to the Emperor what belongs to him, and pay to God
what belongs to God." ²⁶ They could not catch him in a
thing there before the people, so they kept quiet, amazed
at his answer.

The Question about Rising from Death
(Also Matt. 22.23–33; Mark 12.18–27)

²⁷ Some Sadducees came to Jesus. (They are the ones
who say that people will not rise from death.) They asked
him: ²⁸ "Teacher, Moses wrote this law for us: 'If a man
dies and leaves a wife, but no children, that man's brother
must marry the widow so they can have children for the
dead man.' ²⁹ Once there were seven brothers; the oldest
got married, and died without having children. ³⁰ Then the
second one married the woman, ³¹ and then the third; the
same thing happened to all seven — they died without
having children. ³² Last of all, the woman died. ³³ Now,
on the day when the dead are raised to life, whose wife
will she be? All seven of them had married her!"

³⁴ Jesus answered them: "The men and women of this
age marry, ³⁵ but the men and women who are worthy to
be raised from death and live in the age to come do not
marry. ³⁶ They are like angels and cannot die. They are
the sons of God, because they have been raised from death.
³⁷ And Moses clearly proves that the dead will be raised
to life. In the passage about the burning bush he speaks
of the Lord as 'the God of Abraham, the God of Isaac,
and the God of Jacob.' ³⁸ This means that he is the God
of the living, not of the dead — for all are alive to him."
³⁹ Some of the teachers of the Law spoke up, "A good
answer, Teacher!" ⁴⁰ For they did not dare ask Jesus any
more questions.

The Question about the Messiah
(Also Matt. 22.41–46; Mark 12.35–37)

⁴¹ Jesus said to them: "How can it be said that the

Messiah will be the descendant of David? 42 Because David himself says in the book of Psalms:

'The Lord said to my Lord:
Sit here at my right side,
43 Until I put your enemies
As a footstool under your feet.'

44 David, then, called him 'Lord.' How can the Messiah be David's descendant?"

Jesus Warns against the Teachers of the Law
(Also Matt. 23.1–36; Mark 12.38–40)

45 As the whole crowd listened to him, Jesus said to his disciples: 46 "Watch out for the teachers of the Law, who like to walk around in their long robes, and love to be greeted with respect in the market place; who choose the reserved seats in the synagogues and the best places at feasts; 47 who take advantage of widows and rob them of their homes, then make a show of saying long prayers! Their punishment will be all the worse!"

The Widow's Offering
(Also Mark 12.41–44)

21 Jesus looked around and saw rich men dropping their gifts in the Temple treasury, 2 and he also saw a very poor widow dropping in two little copper coins. 3 And he said: "I tell you that this poor widow has really put in more than all the others. 4 For the others offered their gifts from what they had to spare of their riches; but she, poor as she is, gave all she had to live on."

Jesus Speaks of the Destruction of the Temple
(Also Matt. 24.1–2; Mark 13.1–2)

⁵ Some of them were talking about the Temple, how beautiful it looked with its fine stones and the gifts offered to God. Jesus said, ⁶ "All this you see — the time will come when not a single stone here will be left in its place; every one will be thrown down."

Troubles and Persecutions
(Also Matt. 24.3–14; Mark 13.3–13)

⁷ "Teacher," they asked, "when will this be? And what is the sign that will show that the time has come for it to happen?"

⁸ Jesus said: "Watch out; don't be fooled. For many men will come in my name saying, 'I am he!' and, 'The time has come!' But don't follow them. ⁹ Don't be afraid when you hear of wars and revolutions; such things must happen first, but they do not mean that the end is near."
¹⁰ He went on to say: "One country will fight another country, one kingdom will attack another kingdom; ¹¹ there will be terrible earthquakes, famines, and plagues everywhere; there will be awful things and great signs from the sky.
¹² "Before all these things take place, however, you will be arrested and persecuted; you will be handed over to trial in synagogues and be put in prison; you will be brought before kings and rulers for my sake. ¹³ This will be your chance to tell the Good News. ¹⁴ Make up your minds ahead of time not to worry about how you will defend yourselves; ¹⁵ for I will give you such words and wisdom that none of your enemies will be able to resist or deny what you say. ¹⁶ You will be handed over by your parents, your brothers, your relatives, and your friends; they will put some of you to death. ¹⁷ Everyone will hate you because of me. ¹⁸ But not a single hair from your heads will be lost. ¹⁹ Hold firm, for this is how you will save yourselves."

Jesus Speaks of the Destruction of Jerusalem
(Also Matt. 24.15–21; Mark 13.14–19)

²⁰ "When you see Jerusalem surrounded by armies, then you will know that soon she will be destroyed. ²¹ Then those who are in Judea must run away to the hills; those

who are in the city must leave, and those who are out in
the country must not go into the city. ²² For these are 'The
Days of Punishment,' to make come true all that the Scriptures say. ²³ How terrible it will be in those days for
women who are pregnant, and for mothers with little
babies! Terrible distress will come upon this land, and
God's wrath will be against this people. ²⁴ They will be
killed by the sword, and taken as prisoners to all countries,
and the heathen will trample over Jerusalem until their
time is up."

The Coming of the Son of Man
(Also Matt. 24.29–31; Mark 13.24–27)

²⁵ "There will be signs in the sun, the moon, and the
stars. On earth, whole countries will be in despair, afraid
of the roar of the sea and the raging tides. ²⁶ Men will
faint from fear as they wait for what is coming over the
whole earth; for the powers in space will be driven from
their course. ²⁷ Then the Son of Man will appear, coming
in a cloud with great power and glory. ²⁸ When these
things begin to happen, stand up and raise your heads, for
your salvation is near."

The Lesson of the Fig Tree
(Also Matt. 24.32–35; Mark 13.28–31)

²⁹ Then Jesus told them this parable: "Remember the
fig tree and all the other trees. ³⁰ When you see their
leaves beginning to appear you know that summer is near.
³¹ In the same way, when you see these things happening,
you will know that the Kingdom of God is about to come.

³² "Remember this! All these things will take place before the people now living have all died. ³³ Heaven and
earth will pass away; my words will never pass away."

The Need to Watch

³⁴ "Watch yourselves! Don't let yourselves become occu-
pied with too much feasting and strong drink, and the
worries of this life, or that Day may come on you suddenly. ³⁵ For it will come like a trap upon all men over
the whole earth. ³⁶ Be on watch and pray always that you
will have the strength to go safely through all these things
that will happen, and to stand before the Son of Man."

³⁷ Jesus spent those days teaching in the Temple, and

when evening came he would go out and spend the night
on the Mount of Olives. ³⁸ All the people would go to
the Temple early in the morning to listen to him.

The Plot against Jesus
(Also Matt. 26.1–5; Mark 14.1–2; John 11.45–53)

22 The time was near for the Feast of Unleavened
Bread, which is called the Passover. ² The chief
priests and the teachers of the Law were trying to find
some way of killing Jesus; for they were afraid of the
people.

Judas Agrees to Betray Jesus
(Also Matt. 26.14–16; Mark 14.10–11)

³ Then Satan went into Judas, called Iscariot, who was
one of the twelve disciples. ⁴ So Judas went off and spoke
with the chief priests and the officers of the Temple guard
about how he could hand Jesus over to them. ⁵ They were
pleased and offered to pay him money. ⁶ Judas agreed to
it and started looking for a good chance to betray Jesus
to them without the people knowing about it.

Jesus Prepares to Eat the Passover Meal
(Also Matt. 26.17–25; Mark 14.12–21; John 13.21–30)

⁷ The day came during the Feast of Unleavened Bread
when the lambs for the Passover meal had to be killed.
⁸ Jesus sent Peter and John with these instructions: "Go
and get our Passover supper ready for us to eat." ⁹ "Where
do you want us to get it ready?" they asked him. ¹⁰ He
said: "Listen! As you go into the city a man carrying a
jar of water will meet you. Follow him into the house that
he enters, ¹¹ and say to the owner of the house: 'The
Teacher says to you, Where is the room where my disciples
and I will eat the Passover supper?' ¹² He will show you
a large furnished room upstairs, where you will get everything ready." ¹³ They went off and found everything just
as Jesus had told them, and prepared the Passover supper.

The Lord's Supper
(Also Matt. 26.26–30; Mark 14.22–26; 1 Cor. 11.23–25)

¹⁴ When the hour came, Jesus took his place at the table
with the apostles. ¹⁵ And he said to them: "I have wanted
so much to eat this Passover meal with you before I suf-

fer! ¹⁶ For I tell you, I will never eat it until it is given its real meaning in the Kingdom of God." ¹⁷ Then Jesus took the cup, gave thanks to God, and said, "Take this and share it among yourselves; ¹⁸ for I tell you that I will not drink this wine from now on until the Kingdom of God comes." ¹⁹ Then he took the bread, gave thanks to God, broke it, and gave it to them, saying, "This is my body [which is given for you. Do this in memory of me." ²⁰ In the same way he gave them the cup, after the supper, saying, "This cup is God's new covenant sealed with my blood which is poured out for you.]

²¹ "But, look! The one who betrays me is here at the table with me! ²² For the Son of Man will die as God has decided it; but how terrible for that man who betrays him!" ²³ Then they began to ask among themselves which one of them it could be who was going to do this.

The Argument about Greatness

²⁴ An argument came up among the disciples as to which one of them should be thought of as the greatest. ²⁵ Jesus said to them: "The kings of this world have power over their people, and the rulers are called 'Friends of the People.' ²⁶ But this is not the way it is with you; rather, the greatest one among you must be like the youngest, and the leader must be like the servant. ²⁷ Who is greater, the one who sits down to eat or the one who serves him? The one who sits down, of course. But I am among you as one who serves.

²⁸ "You have stayed with me all through my trials; ²⁹ and just as my Father has given me the right to rule, so I will make the same agreement with you. ³⁰ You will eat and drink at my table in my Kingdom, and you will sit on thrones to judge the twelve tribes of Israel."

Jesus Predicts Peter's Denial
(Also Matt. 26.31-35; Mark 14.27-31; John 13.36-38)

³¹ "Simon, Simon! Listen! Satan has received permission to test all of you, as a farmer separates the wheat from the chaff. ³² But I have prayed for you, Simon, that your faith will not fail. And when you turn back to me, you must strengthen your brothers." ³³ Peter answered, "Lord, I am ready to go to prison with you and to die with you!" ³⁴ "I tell you, Peter," Jesus answered, "the

cock will not crow today until you have said three times that you do not know me."

Purse, Bag, and Sword

35 Then Jesus said to them, "When I sent you out that time without purse, bag, or shoes, did you lack anything?" "Not a thing," they answered. 36 "But now," Jesus said, "whoever has a purse or a bag must take it; and whoever does not have a sword must sell his coat and buy one. 37 For I tell you this: the scripture that says, 'He was included with the criminals,' must come true about me. For that which was written about me is coming true." 38 The disciples said, "Look! Here are two swords, Lord!" "That is enough!" he answered.

Jesus Prays
(Also Matt. 26.36–46; Mark 14.32–42)

39 Jesus left and went, as he usually did, to the Mount of Olives; and the disciples went with him. 40 When he came to the place he said to them, "Pray that you will not fall into temptation." 41 Then he went off from them, about the distance of a stone's throw, and knelt down and prayed. 42 "Father," he said, "if you will, take this cup away from me. Not my will, however, but your will be done." [43 An angel from heaven appeared to him and strengthened him. 44 In great anguish he prayed even more fervently; his sweat was like drops of blood, falling to the ground.]

45 Rising from his prayer, he went back to the disciples and found them asleep, so great was their grief. 46 And he said to them, "Why are you sleeping? Rise and pray that you will not fall into temptation."

The Arrest of Jesus
(Also Matt. 26.47-56; Mark 14.43-50; John 18.3-11)

⁴⁷ He was still speaking when a crowd arrived; Judas, one of the twelve disciples, was leading them, and he came up to Jesus to kiss him. ⁴⁸ But Jesus said, "Is it with a kiss, Judas, that you betray the Son of Man?" ⁴⁹ When the disciples who were with Jesus saw what was going to happen, they said, "Shall we strike with our swords, Lord?" ⁵⁰ And one of them struck the High Priest's slave and cut off his right ear. ⁵¹ But Jesus answered, "Enough of this!" He touched the man's ear and healed him.

⁵² Then Jesus said to the chief priests and the officers of the Temple guard and the elders who had come there to get him: "Did you have to come with swords and clubs, as though I were an outlaw? ⁵³ I was with you in the Temple every day, and you did not try to arrest me. But this hour belongs to you and to the power of darkness."

Peter Denies Jesus
(Also Matt. 26.57-58, 69-75; Mark 14.53-54, 66-72; John 18.12-18, 25-27)

⁵⁴ They arrested Jesus and took him away into the house of the High Priest; and Peter followed far behind. ⁵⁵ A fire had been lit in the centre of the courtyard, and Peter joined those who were sitting around it. ⁵⁶ When one of the servant girls saw him sitting there at the fire, she looked straight at him and said, "This man too was with him!" ⁵⁷ But Peter denied it: "Woman, I don't even know him!" ⁵⁸ After a little while, a man noticed him and said, "You are one of them, too!" But Peter answered, "Man,

I am not!" [59] And about an hour later another man insisted strongly: "There isn't any doubt that this man was with him, because he also is a Galilean!" [60] But Peter answered, "Man, I don't know what you are talking about!" At once, while he was still speaking, a cock crowed. [61] The Lord turned around and looked straight at Peter, and Peter remembered the Lord's words, how he had said, "Before the cock crows today, you will say three times that you do not know me." [62] Peter went out and wept bitterly.

Jesus Mocked and Beaten
(Also Matt. 26.67–68; Mark 14.65)

[63] The men who were guarding Jesus made fun of him and beat him. [64] They blindfolded him and asked him, "Who hit you? Guess!" [65] And they said many other insulting things to him.

Jesus before the Council
(Also Matt. 26.59–66; Mark 14.55–64; John 18.19–24)

[66] When day came, the elders of the Jews, the chief priests, and the teachers of the Law met together, and Jesus was brought to their Council. [67] "Tell us," they said, "are you the Messiah?" He answered: "If I tell you, you will not believe me, [68] and if I ask you a question you will not answer me. [69] But from now on the Son of Man will be seated at the right side of the Almighty God." [70] They all said, "Are you, then, the Son of God?" He answered them, "You say that I am." [71] And they said, "We don't need any witnesses! We ourselves have heard his very own words!"

Jesus before Pilate
(Also Matt. 27.1–2, 11–14; Mark 15.1–5; John 18.28–38)

23 The whole group rose up and took Jesus before Pilate, [2] where they began to accuse him: "We caught this man misleading our people, telling them not to pay taxes to the Emperor and claiming that he himself is Christ, a king." [3] Pilate asked him, "Are you the king of the Jews?" "You say it," answered Jesus. [4] Then Pilate said to the chief priests and the crowds, "I find no reason to condemn this man." [5] But they insisted even more strongly, "He is starting a riot among the people with his

teaching! He began in Galilee, went through all of Judea, and now has come here."

Jesus before Herod

⁶ When Pilate heard this he asked, "Is this man a Galilean?" ⁷ When he learned that Jesus was from the region ruled by Herod, he sent him to Herod, who was also in Jerusalem at that time. ⁸ Herod was very pleased when he saw Jesus, for he had heard about him and had been wanting to see him for a long time; he was hoping to see Jesus perform some miracle. ⁹ So Herod asked Jesus many questions, but Jesus did not answer a word. ¹⁰ The chief priests and the teachers of the Law stepped forward and made strong accusations against Jesus. ¹¹ Herod and his soldiers made fun of Jesus and treated him with contempt. They put a fine robe on him and sent him back to Pilate. ¹² On that very day Herod and Pilate became friends; they had been enemies before this.

Jesus Sentenced to Death
(Also Matt. 27.15–26; Mark 15.6–15; John 18.39—19.16)

¹³ Pilate called together the chief priests, the leaders, and the people, ¹⁴ and said to them: "You brought this man to me and said that he was misleading the people. Now, I have examined him here in your presence, and I have not found him guilty of any of the bad things you accuse him of. ¹⁵ Nor did Herod find him guilty, for he sent him back to us. There is nothing this man has done to deserve death. ¹⁶ I will have him whipped, then, and let him go." [¹⁷ At each Passover Feast Pilate had to set free one prisoner for them.] ¹⁸ The whole crowd cried out, "Kill him! Set Barabbas free for us!" ¹⁹ (Barabbas had been put in prison for a riot that had taken place in the city, and for murder.) ²⁰ Pilate wanted to set Jesus free, so he called out to the crowd again. ²¹ But they shouted back, "To the cross with him! To the cross!" ²² Pilate said to them the third time: "But what crime has he committed? I cannot find anything he has done to deserve death! I will have him whipped and set him free." ²³ But they kept on shouting at the top of their voices that Jesus should be nailed to the cross; and finally their shouting won. ²⁴ So Pilate passed the sentence on Jesus that they were asking for. ²⁵ He set free the man they wanted, the

one who had been put in prison for riot and murder, and
turned Jesus over to them to do as they wished.

Jesus Nailed to the Cross
(Also Matt. 27.32–44; Mark 15.21–32; John 19.17–27)

²⁶ They took Jesus away. As they went, they met a
man named Simon, from Cyrene, who was coming into
the city from the country. They seized him, put the cross
on him and made him carry it behind Jesus.

²⁷ A large crowd of people followed him; among them
were some women who were weeping and wailing for him.
²⁸ Jesus turned to them and said: "Women of Jerusalem!
Don't cry for me, but for yourselves and your children.
²⁹ For the days are coming when people will say, 'How
lucky are the women who never had children, who never
bore babies, who never nursed them!' ³⁰ That will be the
time when people will say to the mountains, 'Fall on us!'
and to the hills, 'Hide us!' ³¹ For if such things as these
are done when the wood is green, what will it be like when
it is dry?"

³² They took two others also, both of them criminals,
to be put to death with Jesus. ³³ When they came to the
place called "The Skull," they nailed Jesus to the cross
there, and the two criminals, one on his right and one on
his left. ³⁴ Jesus said, "Forgive them, Father! They don't
know what they are doing." They divided his clothes
among themselves by throwing dice. ³⁵ The people stood
there watching, while the Jewish leaders made fun of him:
"He saved others; let him save himself, if he is the Mes-

siah whom God has chosen!" [36] The soldiers also made fun of him; they came up to him and offered him wine, [37] and said, "Save yourself, if you are the king of the Jews!" [38] These words were written above him: "This is the King of the Jews."

[39] One of the criminals hanging there threw insults at him: "Aren't you the Messiah? Save yourself and us!" [40] The other one, however, rebuked him, saying: "Don't you fear God? Here we are all under the same sentence. [41] Ours, however, is only right, for we are getting what we deserve for what we did; but he has done no wrong." [42] And he said to Jesus, "Remember me, Jesus, when you come as King!" [43] Jesus said to him, "I tell you this: today you will be in Paradise with me."

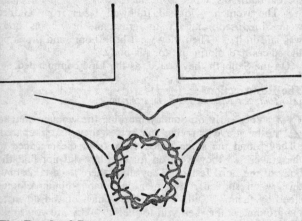

The Death of Jesus
(Also Matt. 27.45–56; Mark 15.33–41; John 19.28–30)

[44] It was about twelve o'clock when the sun stopped shining and darkness covered the whole country until three o'clock; [45] and the curtain hanging in the Temple was torn in two. [46] Jesus cried out in a loud voice, "Father! In your hands I place my spirit!" He said this and died. [47] The army officer saw what had happened, and he praised God, saying, "Certainly he was a good man!" [48] When the people who had gathered there to watch the spectacle saw what happened, they all went back home beating their breasts. [49] All those who knew Jesus per-

sonally, including the women who had followed him from Galilee, stood off at a distance to see these things.

The Burial of Jesus
(Also Matt. 27.57–61; Mark 15.42–47; John 19.38–42)

⁵⁰⁻⁵¹ There was a man named Joseph, from the Jewish town of Arimathea. He was a good and honourable man, and waited for the coming of the Kingdom of God. Although a member of the Council, he had not agreed with their decision and action. ⁵² He went into the presence of Pilate and asked for the body of Jesus. ⁵³ Then he took the body down, wrapped it in a linen sheet, and placed it in a grave which had been dug out of the rock — a grave which had never been used. ⁵⁴ It was Friday, and the Sabbath was about to begin.

⁵⁵ The women who had followed Jesus from Galilee went with Joseph and saw the grave and how Jesus' body was laid in it. ⁵⁶ Then they went back home and prepared the spices and ointments for his body.

On the Sabbath they rested, as the Law commanded.

The Resurrection
(Also Matt. 28.1–10; Mark 16.1–8; John 20.1–10)

24 Very early on Sunday morning the women went to the grave carrying the spices they had prepared. ² They found the stone rolled away from the entrance to the grave, ³ so they went on in; but they did not find the body of the Lord Jesus. ⁴ They stood there uncertain about this, when suddenly two men in bright shining clothes stood by them. ⁵ Full of fear, the women bowed down to the ground, as the men said to them: "Why are you looking among the dead for one who is alive? ⁶ He is not here;

he has risen. Remember what he said to you while he was in Galilee: [7] 'The Son of Man must be handed over to sinful men, be nailed to the cross and be raised to life on the third day.' " [8] Then the women remembered his words, [9] returned from the grave, and told all these things to the eleven disciples and all the rest. [10] The women were Mary Magdalene, Joanna, and Mary the mother of James; they and the other women with them told these things to the apostles. [11] But the apostles thought that what the women said was nonsense, and did not believe them. [12] But Peter got up and ran to the grave; he bent down and saw the grave cloths and nothing else. Then he went back home wondering at what had happened.

The Walk to Emmaus
(Also Mark 16.12–13)

[13] On that same day two of them were going to a village named Emmaus, about seven miles from Jerusalem, [14] and they were talking to each other about all the things that had happened. [15] As they talked and discussed, Jesus himself drew near and walked along with them; [16] they saw him, but somehow did not recognize him. [17] Jesus said to them, "What are you talking about, back and forth, as you walk along?" And they stood still, with sad faces. [18] One of them, named Cleopas, asked him, "Are you the only man living in Jerusalem who does not know what has been happening there these last few days?" [19] "What things?" he asked. "The things that happened to Jesus of Nazareth," they answered. "This man was a prophet, and was considered by God and by all the people to be mighty in words and deeds. [20] Our chief priests and rulers handed him over to be sentenced to death, and they nailed him to the cross. [21] And we had hoped that he would be the one who was going to redeem Israel! Besides all that, this is now the third day since it happened. [22] Some of the women of our group surprised us; they went at dawn to the grave, [23] but could not find his body. They came back saying they had seen a vision of angels who told them that he is alive. [24] Some of our group went to the grave and found it exactly as the women had said, but they did not see him."

[25] Then Jesus said to them: "How foolish you are, how slow you are to believe everything the prophets said!

²⁶ Was it not necessary for the Messiah to suffer these things and enter his glory?" ²⁷ And Jesus explained to them what was said about him in all the Scriptures, beginning with the books of Moses and the writings of all the prophets.

²⁸ They came near the village to which they were going, and Jesus acted as if he were going farther; ²⁹ but they held him back, saying, "Stay with us; the day is almost over and it is getting dark." So he went in to stay with them. ³⁰ He sat at table with them, took the bread, and said the blessing; then he broke the bread and gave it to them. ³¹ Their eyes were opened and they recognized him; but he disappeared from their sight. ³² They said to each other, "Wasn't it like a fire burning in us when he talked to us on the road and explained the Scriptures to us?"

³³ They got up at once and went back to Jerusalem, where they found the eleven disciples gathered together with the others ³⁴ and saying, "The Lord is risen indeed! Simon has seen him!" ³⁵ The two then explained to them what had happened on the road, and how they had recognized the Lord when he broke the bread.

Jesus Appears to His Disciples
(Also Matt. 28.16–20; Mark 16.14–18; John 20.19–23; Acts 1.6–8)

³⁶ While they were telling them this, suddenly the Lord himself stood among them and said to them, "Peace be with you." ³⁷ Full of fear and terror, they thought that they were seeing a ghost. ³⁸ But he said to them: "Why are you troubled? Why are these doubts coming up in your minds? ³⁹ Look at my hands and my feet and see that it is I, myself. Feel me, and you will see, for a ghost doesn't have flesh and bones, as you can see I have." ⁴⁰ He said this and showed them his hands and his feet. ⁴¹ They still could not believe, they were so full of joy and wonder; so he asked them, "Do you have anything to eat here?" ⁴² They gave him a piece of cooked fish, ⁴³ which he took and ate before them.

⁴⁴ Then he said to them: "These are the very things I told you while I was still with you: everything written about me in the Law of Moses, the writings of the prophets, and the Psalms had to come true." ⁴⁵ Then he opened their minds to understand the Scriptures, ⁴⁶ and said to them: "This is what is written: that the Messiah must

suffer and be raised from death on the third day, **47** and that in his name the message about repentance and the forgiveness of sins must be preached to all nations, beginning in Jerusalem. **48** You are witnesses of these things. **49** And I myself will send upon you what my Father has promised. But you must wait in the city until the power from above comes down upon you."

Jesus Is Taken up to Heaven
(Also Mark 16.19–20; Acts 1.9–11)

50 Then he led them out of the city as far as Bethany, where he raised his hands and blessed them. **51** As he was blessing them, he departed from them and was taken up into heaven. **52** They worshipped him and went back into Jerusalem, filled with great joy, **53** and spent all their time in the Temple giving thanks to God.

GOOD NEWS FOR MODERN MAN

The New Testament in Today's English Version

This translation in contemporary language, published originally in the United States by the American Bible Society, has met with wide approval. Over thirty million copies have been sold throughout the world.

Editions available in the United Kingdom published by Collins and Fontana Books.

New Testament T.E.V. illustrated 608 pages

Cloth cover	60p
Rexine cover	£1.35

Published jointly by the British and Foreign Bible Society and the National Bible Society of Scotland in association with Fontana Books.

New Testament illustrated paperback			30p
„ „ paperback without illustrations			20p
Single Books with illustrations			
Matthew	80 pages	4p	
Mark	64 pages	4p	
Luke	84 pages	4p	
John	64 pages	4p	
Philippians	16 pages	2p	
Each Gospel available in large type		12p	
Psalms illustrated paperback 224 pages		20p	